Limerick Lives

Edited by Mary Fennelly

Photography by Michael Martin

The Samaritans

Limerick Lives
is a Samaritans'
fund-raising project,
published as a
contribution to
Limerick's 800th
Charter Celebrations.

1997

LIMERICK
CHARTER
800

Design and Typeset by Intype Ltd., Limerick.

Printed by Leader Print Ltd., Limerick.

Published in hardback in November, 1996, for the Samaritans of Limerick and Tipperary by euroPRomotions, Tait Business Centre, Dominic Street, Limerick, Ireland.
Tel: +353 61 315252/419477
Fax: +353 61 319664
email: europr@iol.ie

ISBN: 0 9529058 0 9

Editor: Mary Fennelly

Photographer: Michael Martin, Limerick, except in the following cases; Vincent Browne's photo by John Carlos, Dublin; Tom Ryan's by Gillian Buckley, Swords, County Dublin; Bill Whelan's by Colm Henry, Dublin; the late Jerry McCabe's, supplied courtesy of Press 22, Limerick and the late Raoul Peter Jackson's from a self-portrait, photographed by Michael Martin.

The moral rights of the writers have been asserted.

Cover Illustration courtesy of Barbara Hartigan, Castleconnell, County Limerick.

Fundraising by euroPRomotions, Limerick.

Design and Typeset by Intype Ltd., Limerick.

Printed by Leader Print Ltd., Limerick.

Foreword

As Mayor of Limerick I am very pleased to write the foreword for this excellent publication and I am confident that it will achieve its dual purpose, *i.e.* the promotion of the Limerick Region and the raising of much needed cash for the Samaritans. *Limerick Lives* is interesting, lively, and 'a must' for Limerick readers in both city and county. While fund-raising is always a difficult task, I believe that this publication represents a novel approach and that it will enjoy the success it undoubtedly deserves.

Recent decades have seen the emergence of the Limerick Region as a major centre for economic, cultural and sporting activities. Even the most cursory glance at Limerick will show a modern, vibrant and growing city together with the necessary and appropriate infrastructural supports. The ongoing growth and expansion of the University of Limerick together with the investment of some £250 million in the redevelopment of the inner city are, perhaps, the most visible manifestations of transformation. The momentum is being maintained with the scheduled opening of the Hunt Museum in 1997 and the imaginative King's Island Development Plan, together with many other initiatives. As Limerick people, we have every reason to be proud of what has been achieved in the past and confident of the future as we now approach the 800th anniversary of the granting of a charter to our ancient city.

Important as these developments are, it must, however, be borne in mind that society is, and must always be, about people and communities. Statistics and analyses will certainly show that, relatively speaking, we have made significant economic progress over the years and that this trend is likely to continue for some time. What cannot be so easily measured is the insecurity, uncertainty and, very often, the real sense of deprivation felt by many who may find it difficult to cope with changing circumstances and adapt to differing demands. The achievement of inclusive economic prosperity, equality of opportunity and a generally caring society is a much more difficult task that planning and implementing economic growth and reshaping our physical surroundings. Success, when viewed in this context, has proven much more elusive.

The scale of certain social problems and the need for prompt and effective responses, represent challenges to which our more conventional commercial or state organisations do not, quite often, respond. This may be as a consequence of a lack of resources, lack of flexibility or, perhaps, even a lack of will. The necessary responses and initiatives have been forthcoming largely from the many voluntary and excellent organisations whose efforts and contributions have proven immeasurable, invaluable and, in every sense, professional and caring. In this regard, I must emphatically state that it would be difficult to envisage any group or organisation playing a more vital and necessary role than the Samaritans. The availability of personnel twenty-four hours a day, seven days a week and fifty-two weeks of the year is, in itself, hugely demanding. When one adds to this the crucial and highly specialised nature of the helpline service, it becomes quite evident that the level of personal commitment provided by each and every one of the Samaritans is well beyond what one might reasonably (or even unreasonably!) expect. The Friends of the Samaritans, for their part, are engaged in ongoing fund-raising campaigns to ensure that the resources necessary for such an organisation are available. Our society owes a great debt to these voluntary workers who give so selflessly and generously of their time, expertise and commitment.

As Mayor of Limerick I salute the efforts of the Friends of the Samaritans and acknowledge and commend the tremendous work of the Samaritans.

Long may your excellent work continue.

Councillor Kieran O'Hanlon,
Mayor of Limerick

Bíonn súil le muir, ach ní bhíonn súil le tír.

There is hope from the sea,
but none from the grave.

Old Irish Proverb

Preface

It was a dark, cold night in January 1994. A newly-formed group, the Friends of the Samaritans, had gathered in the basement of 20 Barrington Street, Limerick. Their task: to raise the £34,000 needed to clear the outstanding mortgage on this self-same building, the Samaritans' new centre in Limerick City. This was to happen in parallel to regular fund-raising activities, required for the day-to-day running of the Samaritans' twenty-four hour befriending service to the suicidal and despairing. Thus began *Limerick Lives*.

During the weeks and months that followed, the Friends - Anne Corver, Margaret Johnston, Kieran Joyce, Agnes Keane, Pat Laffan, Jim Larkin, Michael Martin, Sean Murphy, Eddie O'Neill, Clem O'Sullivan, Annette Shanahan, Catherine Slater and myself - met at regular intervals to tease out the format that this new book would take.

By the end of 1994, the plan, which benefited in the early stages from the input of Tim O'Brien, was in place. Over three hundred people - interesting characters from Limerick City and County - were to be invited for inclusion in *Limerick Lives,* subject to a sponsorship of £350 backing up each entry. At this stage, Michael Martin agreed to be the photographer for the project, and I took on the role of project manager.

1995 was spent laying solid foundations to ensure success. This involved lining up a professional printer and designer for the job, awarded to Limerick firms Leader Print Ltd. and Intype Ltd. respectively.

In January, 1996, mock-ups, produced, thanks to the co-operation of Helen and Tom O'Donnell and journalist, Dymphna Bracken, together with personalised invitations, were sent to the proposed candidates for the book. A publicity campaign was launched to encourage nominations and offers of sponsorship from the general public. By Easter, as a result of intensive telephone follow-up with the able assistance of Caroline Roche and Helena McMurdo, enough money - a combination of personal donations and corporate sponsorship - had been taken in to allow production of *Limerick Lives* to commence.

By September, everything was nearly in place, with the photographic work completed, and input from nearly all of the forty-plus contributing writers on hand and already typeset. Contributions by Limerick artist, Barbara Hartigan, by way of a specially created illustration for the book cover and the invaluable advice and guidance of Seán Spellissy in finalising copy for the book, helped a great deal. Edel Cassidy's and Eleanor McGranahan's kind offer to work with the Friends to co-ordinate the book launch event was also most welcome during the busy weeks preceding publication.

After production costs, £9,000 profit was left from the *Limerick Lives* sponsorship moneys as a lump sum payment off the outstanding mortgage. Profit from the sale of the two thousand copies is expected to go a long way towards clearing the remainder, so as a fund-raising venture, *Limerick Lives* cannot lose.

In addition to the important financial injection to the Samaritans' mortgage funds, it is hoped that *Limerick Lives* will also generate a new sense of pride and hope amongst the citizens of Limerick City and County in the advent of the 800th Charter Celebrations in 1997. The book is not intended to be a *Who's Who,* but rather a collection of cheerful photographs and short stories on seventy-five different individuals or groups, whose only common link is Limerick. In the same way as the book features people from all walks of life, so too does the Samaritans' work benefit individuals from all sections of our community. Making a wider circle of people aware of the Samaritans and what they do, so that they might think of them again at a time of desperation, is another important role which *Limerick Lives* will play.

It is a great delight and relief to see *Limerick Lives* finally come together. It has been a long and challenging project, but a very rewarding one, which has brought together the talents and efforts, goodwill and financial contributions of hundreds of people. In thanking all of these, I would like to give special mention to Michele Dunford for her valuable day-to-day assistance on the project, and to my family and friends for their encouragement along the way, most especially my parents, Marie, my greatest friend and supporter on earth, and my late father Mick, my guiding star in Heaven.

Mary Fennelly

Contents

*Recently deceased.

The Samaritans wish to thank
the following journalists and writers,

Leonard Burke
Dymphna Bracken
Eileen Brophy
Tommy Browne
Canon Brendan Cannellan
Niall Cantrell
Siobhán Colgan
Claire Connolly Doyle
Aidan Corr
Bernie English
Mary Fennelly
Monseigneur John Flemming
Harry Greensmyth
Cathy Halloran
Frank Hamilton
Tom Healy
Cathy Jackson
Mal Keaveney
Lynne Kelleher
Billy Kelly
Ron Kirwan
Linda Lane
Marian Malone

Kieran McConville
Brian McLaughlin
James O'Brien
Dónal Ó Murchú
Seán Murphy
Anna Nolan
Valerie O'Connor
Trish O'Dea
Michael O'Flaherty
John O'Shaughnessy
Fr. John O'Shea
Eugene Phelan
Eleanor Plunkett
Norma Prendiville
Arthur Quinlan
Brian Quinlivan
Rose Rushe
Noel Smith
Valerie Sweeney
Dermot Walsh
Mary Wilson
Katherine Woulfe

who gave of their time and talents to write the

Limerick Lives

Interviews

Noel Alfred

Ask the kids from Adare Youth Club what the age-spread of the membership is and they will tell you twelve to twenty-one. Ask the community in Adare and they will confirm that the club has brightened the lives of both young and old - an achievement which has won them the prestigious Community Development Youth Work Award from the National Youth Federation.

Founded in 1968, the club is the oldest of its kind in Limerick and one of the oldest in the country. With ninety to one hundred members, it's a club full of life and bright ideas and an organisation where youngsters learn what it means to be part of their own community.

Come Christmas, youngsters from the club spend up to three days stringing thousands of bulbs on one of the biggest and brightest trees in the county to drive the Winter gloom from the streets of Adare.

And every child in the area looks forward to a free, no-holds-barred kiddies' Christmas bash, hosted by and paid for by the members of the club.

"For the last seventeen years, the club has unfailingly raised the £3,000 necessary to bring festive cheer to Adare. Local business people return the youngsters' interest and efforts by supporting their fundraising and individuals often stop leaders and members in the street to offer cash towards the cost," says former club president, Noel Alfred.

But the club's involvement with local projects is much more than an annual effort. "If there's dirty work to be done, people know they can ask the Youth Club", jokes Noel. "Whether it's a clean-up for the tidy towns or something messy that needs dealing with, the community knows that they can call on us".

Noel feels that the award - presented in 1994 - was not for anything the club did in one year, but for on-going involvement running fund-raising stay-awakes and discos, hosting the Christmas party and helping at events like the St. Patrick's Day Parade. The members also raise money for a charity to send children to Lourdes and to help the three schools in the area.

"A lot of young people need some way of fitting in - something to give them purpose," says Noel. "I think where we succeed is in having a family atmosphere approach. Some other clubs organise along the lines of a school - we don't do that".

> "It's not just a club - it's more a frame of mind. For all of us, it's a stepping stone to life."

Leaders, James Dillon, Joey O'Brien and Kevin and Derek Griffin are rightly proud of the club's achievements. They have been Munster champions in the national disco dancing competitions three times, runners-up in the All Ireland chess championships and runners-up in the National group singing event organised by the federation.

They also produce and stage three short plays and a musical show every year, with the members scripting the lion's share of the show.

An on-going programme of games, quizzes, discos and organised outings up to three nights a week is set to continue into the future. Noel, who has just retired, explains: "There are already young members coming up who want to be involved in the committee. It's the members' club. Each new batch of leaders takes the best of what has been learned over the years and improves on it. That's how Adare Youth Club keeps going".

In conversation with Bernie English

Maggie Alton

"I was a hewer of wood and a drawer of water," says Maggie Alton of her life's work on a smallholding in the tiny village of Glenosheen.

Now, at ninety-three and still healthy, Maggie is the oldest living Palatine in the county, if not the country.

A tiny, neat lady, Maggie's story is in one sense the story of all Palatines, governed as it was by her love of her garden, her simple, hard-working habits and her commitment to family. But Maggie is also one of the last links in the story of the Palatines in Glenosheen - a link that goes back to 1761 when the then landlords, the Olivers', invited some of the German families on to the estate.

The first Palatines, from the German Rhine-Pfalz region, had settled on the Southwell estate at Rathkeale in 1712, their industriousness, their husbandry skills and crafts making them exceptional tenants. In Glenosheen, too, the Palatines settled in quietly, adding a new melody to an already rich culture and imposing their own order on the lush, soft landscape.

And the ties with the Castle Oliver estate continued over generations. Maggie's grandfather was a gardener on the estate. She herself grew up in a cottage owned by the estate and has clear memories of the big house, Castle Oliver. "At Christmas time," she says, "Mrs Frances Trench used to invite all the tenants' children to a party. She was very kind to children. There was nobody excluded," says Maggie. "We loved the parties, all the buns and the little oranges. We would be talking about it for ages after."

Maggie sang in the local Church of Ireland choir and attended the local Protestant school, where she was sometimes put in charge of the little ones and hoped herself to become a teacher one day.

But as the eldest in the family, she was required to work and shortly after leaving school she began working as a nanny with an English family in Bournemouth. "It was very different," she recalls. Other posts followed, some in Ireland, but with the outbreak of World War II, Maggie returned home. "I wanted to come home and settle down in my own little village if possible," she says. Her mother, by then, was failing in health and a younger brother and sister required constant care.

Thus began a new chapter in Maggie's life, as they settled in the cottage that is still her home fifty-seven years later. "I never regretted it, not for one minute," she says.

Her growing up was happy. "I thought it was lovely. It was very quiet and simple. We just knew we were Palatines. It didn't make me feel very different."

It was a life of unremitting toil, punctuated only by the seasons and the small diversions of rural life - the long walk to Kilfinane and back, the visits to neighbours. But always there was her garden and her reading. "I love my garden," Maggie says simply. Sweet William, roses, Michaelmas daisies, phlox - she loves all the flowers and is still proud that she can read without glasses.

Her life is quieter now, but "I like when I stand up there at the sink looking over to the Galtee Mountains," she says. Glenosheen is her world, a place where everybody "has a word for you," where you "sort of grow into" your neighbours and where it is very peaceful".

"I am very thankful to God for his goodness," she says, "that I was able to look after the others when they weren't able to look after themselves and that I was able to do my bit of gardening."

In conversation with Norma Prendiville

Jack Bourke

Limerick you're a Lady - the Anthem of the City of Limerick is how Jack Bourke fondly describes his most beloved adopted city. Jack Bourke arrived from Dublin over forty years ago and fell in love with the *Lady* that is Limerick. He also fell in love with Monica (*née* McHugh), grandniece of the Bishop of Derry, Charles McHugh and kinswoman of John Hume M.P. Jack and Monica had four children. They now have five grandchildren ranging from eighteen to one year, all of whom are living in the City of Limerick.

Jack is the son of the famous theatrical impresario, Lorcan Bourke, and is either related to or associated with the most prestigious and famous theatrical personae in the country among whom are: Peadar Kearney (1893-1942), author of *the Soldier's Song;* Kevin Barry (1902-1920) of patriot fame; Brendan Behan (1923-1964); Seamus DeBurca, playwright and historian; Eamon Andrews; Kevin Bourke, managing director of Bourke Strand Electric; costume designer, Kotchie Bourke of P.J. Bourke Theatrical Custumiers; Gerry Ryan of R.T.E. fame and Pete St. John.

> "I would like to think that I made my contribution to the renaissance of Limerick as a city."

Jack came to Limerick after his father Lorcan bought the City Theatre. A very young man, Jack was sent down to manage this theatre and did so with vigour and enthusiasm. At that time the 1000-seat theatre was a resounding success and was "first" with many shows from Britain, Dublin and Limerick. With the passage of time the theatrical business became more and more problematic: "Times changed with the advent of TV."

In 1967 Jack was elected to the City Council after being coaxed into running by the then Minister for Education, Donogh O'Malley T.D. Jack became mayor in 1968 which he describes as one of the proudest moments of his life. While still operating the city theatre, Jack performed his onerous duties as mayor with great verve and panache, which by any standards must have been extremely taxing. "When one is young and full of vitality its not so difficult". Jack had the honour of being Limerick's first citizen from 1968 to 1969 and again from 1986 to 1987.

Chairman of the Mid-Western Board for over fourteen years, a position he greatly cherishes, Jack talks with great enthusiasm and pride about the improvements in Limerick's health service and especially of the expansion of the Limerick Regional Hospital, with which he is proud to be associated. The current expansion will have nine new hospital theatres and will have only the fourth formal cardiologist to be positioned anywhere in this country apart from the universities and the medical teaching schools. Consequently, Limerick will now have the first cardiologist outside of Dublin, Galway and Cork. Jack also claims that an extremely advantageous and rewarding £150 million will have been spent on the hospital by the time it is finished. "The timing is brilliant; it will bring the Limerick Regional Hospital into a position to serve the Mid-West region of a population of 320,000 people, right into the 21st century and bang on time".

He is also delighted to see the propitious partnership between the University of Limerick and the Health Board in the training of nurses and he remembers with great pride how as a young mayor in 1968 he lead a deputation to meet the then Minister for Education, Mr. Brian Lenihan T.D. to demand that the college in question get "University Status".

In conversation with Eileen Brophy

Sr. Joan Bowles

Sr. Joan Bowles has spent her adult life helping young people in Limerick. Sr. Joan was born in Doon, County Limerick where she attended the Convent of Mercy before joining the Mercy Order.

Her first role as a nun was that of primary school teacher, during which time she worked voluntarily as a leader with youth clubs in the Limerick area. Up to the present day, Mainline Youthwork - offering leadership and development opportunities for volunteer leaders and educational and recreational programmes for young people throughout Limerick City and County - has remained one of her top priorities.

Following her time teaching in primary school Sr. Joan went to London where she did further studies and became a remedial teacher. From there she went to Swansea University. On graduating, she returned to Ireland and set up the Limerick Youth Service.

Sr. Joan admits that she was always interested in working with young people and, though the Sisters of Mercy had always been very involved in teaching and nursing, they had not, at this time, been involved specifically in any type of youth work. Once she had begun her work in this area, however, the order became, and remains her most fervent supporter.

Many of the young people with whom she works have, for a variety of reasons, missed out on basic educational and social opportunities. Large numbers had dropped out of the school system and feel they have no role in life and it is Sr. Joan's opinion that we must find a niche for each one of them.

"It can be harrowing dealing with some of these sixteen to eighteen year olds at the centre", she adds, "but what we have here is a fantastic staff who are really committed to the needs of these youngsters".

At present Limerick Youth Service caters for 120 young people on full time programmes, but Sr. Joan feels that an expansion in residential facilities is crucial to back-up the day time programmes at the centre.

Sr. Joan believes that the social skills of the young people at the centre benefit greatly from dealing with others. One of her main innovations at Limerick Youth Service was the setting up of a number of projects offering practical skills training, which are open to the general public. "It is a service to the public", says Sister Joan, "through which the youngsters are learning while gaining in self-esteem, which is often very low in the beginning".

> "Limerick people are friendly and warm and willing to help, and since I started twenty-three years ago, nobody ever refused to help me."

Limerick Youth Service, though in receipt of funds from a variety of sources, is still very dependent on voluntary donations, and Sr. Joan admits that drumming up funds is getting more difficult every year, as their needs increase.

She admits also that it saddens her when people portray Limerick in a bad light. "In my experience", she points out, "there is an extraordinary voluntary commitment to the city by the public, they are the most generous people I have ever come across. For the size of the population they are quite remarkable".

Her hope for the Limerick Youth Service could also be applicable to her hope for the city; "Let this place be a place of hope and a place of encouragement".

In conversation with Trish O'Dea

Vincent Browne

For nearly thirty years, Vincent Browne has been at the cutting edge of Irish journalism. It is a passion which still consumes him. "The role of journalism," he says, "is to hold the institutions of power accountable." Sharp, keenly political, trenchant in his opinions and acute in his analysis he has played his own role within that context and built up a considerable reputation in a tough profession.

"I have had a great time," says the man who reported on the Russian invasion of Czechoslovakia. He spent three years as Northern News Editor for *The Irish Press* and broke new ground in investigative journalism with the setting up of *Magill* in 1977.

Editor of *The Sunday Tribune* until he was ousted in a boardroom coup in 1994, he has continued to make his mark with columns in *The Irish Times* and *The Sunday Times* and returned to the airwaves this autumn with his own current affairs radio programme on RTE. He is also planning to revive *Magill*.

Vincent Browne still hates shopping though - a leftover from his childhood in the County Limerick village of Broadford.

"I developed a lifelong antipathy to shopping during trips to Limerick. Buying even a pair of shoes was an endless task for my mother. It involved trailing around from shop to shop, fitting on countless pairs of shoes, rejecting them all and going on to the next shop. Finally, she would negotiate taking a pair on 'appro'."

Growing up in Broadford was great. It was a place of

"It has been great fun. I have been doing things that I would have wanted to do even if I were not paid for it. It is great to combine work and play."

friends yet "every one of those in my class, bar myself, emigrated. Nobody other than myself from that class went through secondary school and several were brighter and more academically successful than I had been."

"In many ways I regret that I was sent to boarding school," I lost contact with Broadford. But there were some gains of course, including the friendships I made that otherwise I would not have made."

Vincent Browne does not subscribe to the concept of county distinctiveness. "I don't have a sense of Limerick people being very different," he says. For all that, he admits that in sport, "I wish Cork badly almost irrespective of who they play". And despite almost forty years in Dublin, he says: "I don't ever see myself or think of myself as a Dubliner."

There are quirks to the Limerick personality, he adds, "a contrast between a certain wildness and a profound reverence."

And the two don't always sit together well. "The confraternity on the one hand, the rugby on the other - the two clash," he says.

He returns to Broadford with his wife, Jean, and daughters, Emma and Julia, several times a year to visit his brother David and family and to renew some close friendships.

And one day, he hopes to finish the history of Broadford, which his father, Séamus, was working on before his death.

In conversation with Norma Prendiville

Ciaran Carey

Courtesy of a point in time added on by Ciarán Carey, Limerick put paid to Clare's ambition of retaining the titles which placed them on top of the hurling world in 1995 and sent Limerick's hopes rocketing in 1996, eventually leading to a confrontation with Wexford in the All-Ireland final.

That winning point, coming just after Limerick had drawn level in a hectic Munster semi-final, will take its place in hurling history alongside any of the famous scores registered by players such as Christy Ring, Mick Mackey, Jimmy Smyth, Nicky Rackard, Eddie Kehir, or any of the great score getters, present or past. The huge home support at the Gaelic grounds on that scorching June Sunday, would have gone home delighted with a draw, but not Ciarán Carey.

Ciarán, made the hurling headlines at local level in 1984, when at the age of fourteen, he lined out at corner forward with Patrickswell in the county minor hurling final against fellow parishioners Ballybrown. He made a fantastic contribution to his side's victory - their first at this level. Incidently, Patrickswell also contested the 1996 minor final, captained by Ciarán's brother, Paul.

Playing at midfield after being switched with Mike Houlihan, he faced a long Clare clearance - made a superb catch - a breathtaking solo run - then fired over a point to write his name on the pages of Irish sporting history.

Since his introduction to hurling in the playing greens of his native Patrickswell, Ciarán was marked as a player of real potential. With the local school and under-age teams, he was recognised as a hurler of the future. His father Pakie, a former Patrickswell hurler watched his son move up the ranks to gain a place among the greats and realise every boy's ambition - to lead his county around the hallowed sod of Croke Park on All-Ireland final day. This he did on the first Sunday of September, 1996, leading Limerick, with Martin Storey at the head of Wexford.

Now aged twenty-six, he is married to Miriam, a daughter of Phil Bennis, himself a holder of an All-Ireland medal with Limerick in 1973. They have a son and daughter, Sarah four and Barry one.

The holder of two Munster medals, a national league medal, various county championships with Patrickswell, All-Star awards, sports stars with weekly newspapers, recognition by various institutions and a county captaincy, Ciarán has come a long way since he first lined out at senior level with his county in the 1988 national league against Dublin.

There was a time in the not too distant past, when the role of a captain was nothing more than an honorary one. Lead the parade, call the toss and if lucky, collect the cup, were the main functions of a captain. This trend has changed, particularly, with Ciarán Carey. He has proven what it takes to be a leader. Skilled, clever, well-versed in all facets of hurling, he is the ideal captain.

The Limerick team of the nineties has gone down as one of the best to come out of the county. The ultimate prize of an All-Ireland crown was swept from their grasp in the concluding moments of the 1994 final. Ciarán Carey, was one of the players to suffer the anguish of defeat on that occasion, but like all great sportsmen, he quickly overcame the disappointment of defeat, not just to play for his resurgent county, but to captain it as well in 1996.

In conversation with Harry Greensmyth

Patrick Cassidy

Patrick Cassidy is widely recognised as Ireland's most important young composer. His music has been performed in France, Britain and the United States, as well as in Ireland. His compositions reflect a deep-felt understanding of ancient Irish music combined with a thorough knowledge of formal classical European forms.

Patrick, started his piano lessons at the age of seven. After graduating from the University of Limerick in 1986, he spent five years working for Irish Marketing Surveys as chief statistician. Most of the money he earned was spent on music books.

His family moved a number of times when Patrick was growing up, and he attended five different schools, so perhaps it's no wonder that he was drawn to the instrument of the wanderer - the Irish harp. He is the son of Colm and Kathleen Cassidy, who own Cassidy's Pharmacies in Limerick.

"When I'm writing a piece of music, I become absorbed in it, so I don't have time to practise. I don't write for a particular performer, and I don't write it for myself to perform. Anyone should be able to pick up the music and play it."

It was not until 1989, that Patrick Cassidy the composer came to prominence with the release of his debut album *Cruit*, an arrangement of Ireland's seventeenth and eighteenth century harpers for baroque ensemble where he himself was the soloist on the Irish harp. In its haunting strains, the young composer found an instrument that could perfectly express Ireland's mythical and historical themes.

Four years later in 1993, Patrick released *The Children of Lir*. This album was recorded by the London Symphony Orchestra and the Tallis Choir and achieved gold status in Ireland.

In 1994, the BAFTA Awards featured Patrick's music on a retrospective of Ireland's contribution to film. In fact Patrick himself wrote the music score for the feature film, *Broken Harvest,* which opened the Dublin Film Festival that same year.

The composer's next work, *Famine Remembrance,* a symphony for orchestra and choir, was premiered at New York's Saint Patrick's Cathedral with Angelica Houston delivering the narration. His latest composition, *Deirdre of the Sorrows,* is based on the *Annals of Ulster.*

As Patrick Cassidy's reputation grows, he knows he is catering for a limited market, but refuses to be constricted by traditional bias.

Composing is an intensive task, so Patrick has found that he has less and less time to dedicate to his playing. This change suits him, as he feels that composing is what he is happiest doing.

In 1996 Patrick received the Chairman's Award from the University of Limerick, for his outstanding work since graduating. As one of his close friends once remarked; "In an odd, detached way, Patrick Cassidy is a genius."

In conversation with Tom Healy

Willie Cauley

Most artists like to see their paintings in a good light, but artist and traveller, Willie Cauley, is content to breathe life into his canvas by candlelight.

He took up a paintbrush on his thirtieth birthday when a friend gave him a palette and paints. "It was my friend, Limerick poet Maureen Sparling, who first called me the "Candlelight Painter", and it stuck! The reason is quite simple. I live in a caravan with no electricity. When my kids are asleep, I light a candle and start painting. I like the mixture of light and shadows on the canvas from the flickering light".

Willie attributes part of his success as an artist to not being afraid to try out lots of techniques and colour combinations. He recalls on one occasion, snipping a piece from his fringe and wrapping it in silver paper to create a different texture with the paints. "At this, my poor cat squealed and made a leap out the door, afraid, it seemed, that she would be the next victim!"

Although he travelled around a bit in his youth, the forty-two-year-old, who was born in Bedford Row, always returned to Limerick. He now lives along the banks of the canal in Limerick with his wife, Brigid, and seven children. "I am very proud to be a Limerick man, especially when I see my paintings hanging in various places around the city".

Willie began drawing during his sporadic periods at primary school. "One of the Christian Brothers told me I was good enough to be an artist. I used to go to school for a few months and then we would take to the road again. I educated myself through reading books and papers while we were travelling".

He calls halting sites 'concentration camps': "I couldn't stand living surrounded by nothing but walls, but my main aim is to bring up my children in a house."

When the painter was sixteen, he approached a Franciscan priest about joining the order, but was told, he wasn't educated enough. "He wouldn't even let me be a missionary, but I had met my wife soon afterwards, so I lost interest".

Much of his childhood was spent travelling around the countryside in a horse-drawn caravan. "There were sixteen children in my family, so it got very overcrowded. It was incredibly tough", says Willie. "We slept in an old tent on a bed of straw. I often woke up to feel water seeping down my back. When I was ten, three men arrived up to our camp in Galway with flaming torches and told us, they would burn us out if we didn't leave".

Willie concedes that there is still a lot of discrimination against travellers. "I think it is a pity that a greater effort isn't made to create a better understanding between the settled and travelling communities. This can only happen, however, if children from both groups go to the same schools, take part in the same sports and learn to accept each other's ways from an early age". Six of Willie's own children attend 'regular' schools in Limerick, while his oldest daughter, Julianne, is in Lisnagry. "All are doing well", he reports with a sense of pride, "and are happy".

Unknown to many, the Candlelight Painter has also penned some poetry in his time. One of his most touching verses is about a Limerick character, *Old Rosy*, who died on the streets of the city some years back. "I wanted to make people more aware of the hardship faced by the homeless and create greater tolerance", he explains, following the recitation.

In conversation with Lynne Kelleher and Mary Fennelly

Angela Collins O'Mahoney

In the last thirty years Dr. Angela Collins O'Mahoney has scaled the heights of success that others only dream about. A self-made woman, not only can the ever-active mother of four claim the title of sole female steeplejack in Ireland (and by all accounts, the world), but she was also the establisher and managing director of two major Irish and International steeplejack companies; was the founding force behind the Landscape Game and Leisure Centre at Clonlara; and returned life to the historic Anglers Rest Bar and Restaurant, Doonass, which had lain in ruin for over 10 years.

Born and raised in Kilkishen, County Clare, Angela's first step into the steeplejack business came in the early '60s. Straight from completing a commercial course at McNamara's High School in Limerick's Crescent, she took up a position as 'girl Friday' with Lynch's Steeplejack Company on St. Joseph's Street, remaining there for six years until her employer died.

In 1966 she married John O'Mahoney, a guard stationed at the then William Street Garda Station and a native of Millstreet, County Cork. She met John while he was waiting to put a ticket on her car, but he's paid for that since as they celebrated thirty years of marriage last August!

It was while her husband was stationed at Caherconlish that Angela met up with the previous employees of her old steeplejack job. Deciding then to form her own steeplejack company, she asked them to come and work for her.

"During the first few years I worked on sites like the E.S.B. chimney in Tarbert which was 420 feet high, and the Communications Tower at Inch, 350 feet high ... and I enjoyed every moment of it!"

The first and only woman steeplejack on the Emerald Isle, Angela and her company caught the interest of the nation and work began to flow in. Appearances on the *Late Late Show,* coupled with numerous newspaper articles, made the company a household name and eventually John decided to resign from the Gardaí to help his wife with the business.

Success followed success and in the early '70s, Collins Steeplejacks met an American company, Electronic Space Systems Corporation, and, with the help of the I.D.A., formed a second company with them called Essco-Collins, which was to manufacture radomes (large structures which protect radar antenna systems from the elements) and install them throughout the world.

The achievements within her own career and her huge commitment to both local and world communities have not slid by unnoticed. In 1980 the high-flying operator was chosen by a prestigious panel of journalists as Irish Business Woman of the Year.

"Life has been very good to me," she now says, "and I have many happy memories of getting our first contracts at Clover Meats and then moving to Mattersons, to Ranks and from there to the Limerick Clothing Factory. I remember replacing the cross on the Redemptorist Church; we cleaned the front of the Franciscan Church in 1969; worked in the Dominican Church, St. Munchin's, St. Mary's Church of Ireland; and carried out extensive repairs to St. John's Cathedral. We also worked on St. Michael's, the Augustinian Church and all the convents in Limerick. So, you see, Limerick has been very good to me."

In conversation with Siobhan Colgan

Mickey Condon

Virtues far outshone any failings of the late Mickey Condon, who is best described as having been a complex person and a true "character". He possessed a wide-ranging knowledge of, and interest in, all facets of life. He was imbued with a deep love of family, country, nature, friends and above all Gaelic games, especially hurling which he aptly described "as the fastest and most scientific team field game in the world". "It is a game of art and skill, in truth 'an art form'," Mickey claimed.

Married to the former Bride Moloney, Mickey was extremely proud to be the seventh generation of the Condon family to farm on the beloved homestead at Fanningstown, Fedamore. They had three children - John (Seán), surely the most underrated hurler ever to wear the Limerick jersey, Michael (Haulie) and daughter, Anne.

Mickey first made an impact on the hurling scene in the mid-20s with his native Fedamore on a team that carved its own little niche in hurling history by winning the 1926 County Junior Hurling Championship at the expense of Newcastlewest. A year later, they won Fedamore's last Limerick Senior Hurling Championship crown and beat Croom in the 1928 final.

Mickey was a member of the Shannonside selection that won the 1927 Munster Junior Hurling Championship by beating Clare but was surprisingly ousted by Meath in the All-Ireland semi-final at Portlaoise. He recalls that Limerick were short three of their best players for that month, because they were clerical students in Maynooth and would not be allowed out of college once the holidays were over!

Having won an Oznam Cup medal with Fedamore in 1928, Mickey became a regular on the Limerick senior team during the golden days of Limerick hurling. He received the game's highest accolade in the Silver Jubilee Year of 1934, when Timmy Ryan led Limerick to victory over Dublin in a replay after

> "I think the Irish people owe a deep debt of gratitude to the G.A.A. It was the association more than anything else that helped to bring people together again after the Civil War. The bitterness left when both sides began to play on the one team."

Mickey Condon had played a major role in an exciting drawn encounter.

The American Tour in 1936 by the Limerick hurlers and Cavan footballers held happy memories for Mickey Condon. "It was simply marvellous", he recalled. Limerick played New York twice in Yankee Stadium and also in Boston to win the coveted Reeves Cup. "We were five days on the *SS Manhattan* Liner and the whole trip lasted six weeks". Amazingly, Mickey's last game for Limerick was in London on Whit Sunday 1936. One of his proud possessions from that nostalgic occasion was his boat ticket from Dun Laoghaire to Hollyhead, which cost the princely sum of 47/6 or in today's monetary terms - £2.37½p!

Mickey Condon recalled a funny incident from his first game at the New Field - now known as the Gaelic Grounds on the Ennis Road - in a tournament game between Fedamore and Newport with Canon Hamilton as referee. The evening was very gloomy as the ball dropped into the Fedamore goalmouth, who were leading by two points. Tom Shinney dived for the ball, but it got lost in the mud! Everybody was searching and finally Newport's Pat Ryan pointed to the ball in the back of the net. The referee allowed a goal, and Newport won by a point! Many moons later Pat Ryan admitted he found the ball in the mud and threw it into the net!

Mickey Condon celebrated his ninetieth birthday with his family and friends in Ard na Rí nursing home near Bruff on June 29th, 1996, but sadly died a week later on July 6th and is laid to rest in his beloved Fedamore.

Nor Shall Your Glory Be Forgot; While fame her record keeps; Or honour points the hollowed spot; Where valour proudly sleeps.

Solas na bhflaitheas dá ainm uasail

Remembered by Sean Murphy

Tony Connolly

"Limerickmen in their own discreet way are quite fashion-conscious, an old influence", according to leading menswear retailer, Tony Connolly, "from the days when production flourished in the city's three clothing factories, then employing some two thousand workers".

Reflecting on those halcyon times, when the trade locally was renowned for style and quality world-wide and the tailors' craftsmanship superb, Tony Connolly says: "Of course the clothing industry has had a tremendous tradition in Limerick".

However, despite this era of sartorial elegance he explains, it was inevitable that clothing factories would not survive when competition emerged from countries where labour was far cheaper.

Mention of the supremacy of Saville Row tailoring and Tony muses: "You'd want to be a very rich man to buy a suit there now. The trade has all changed ... most suits and jackets nowadays are bought off the peg. Ready-mades are so skilfully made, they can be altered to fit the customer", he explains.

"A Limerickman is a superb judge of quality. He'll know immediately if a suit is well made."

Although most of the leading firms in Ireland, that catered for the made-to-measure trade are no longer in business, Tony is proud of the ones that managed to survive and prosper, particularly Limerick's Shannon Clothing Company. Magee's of Donegal also continue to fly the flag and are exporting their garments throughout Europe.

Tony Connolly served a three-year apprenticeship to the drapery business in Kingston's in Patrick Street, in the premises which is now one of his own five shops - four in Limerick and one in Clonmel. His first venture into business on his own was at Upper William Street in 1970.

Limerick business is buoyant at present and has been for some time. "It always is when interest rates are low", according to Tony. "When rates spiral, the rag trade is one of the first victims. First of all the mortgages have to be paid", reflects the successful businessman.

On men's fashion today, his own preference is for the single-breasted jacket but he is of course acutely conscious of his customers' tastes.

Tony Connolly agrees that the double-breasted suit, which made a spectacular comeback about five years ago is still very popular. "There's a great selection of men's fashions now on offer, with many men going for the more casual outfit. Of course fashion is constantly changing and Limerick is always up with the new trends," he smiles.

Interestingly Tony points out, that in general a Limerickman buys one suit every year, along with the casuals. "There are men, of course, who for professional or business reasons buy up to three. There's always the special purchase of a suit too for the big family occasion - a wedding, confirmation and so on".

A city man who now lives with his wife, Rose and six children in Ballyneety, Tony is a firm believer in apprenticeship training for assistants. "The training may not be the same as in the old days", he says. "The man with the tape around his shoulders ready to measure the customer for his new suit was very important then. Nowadays however, assistants are trained to assist and advise customers in style and colour co-ordination".

Tony Connolly believes there are many opportunities for young people in business today to open on their own. "There's always a niche to be exploited. Nothing ever remains the same in the clothing business, which is why it continues to be such an exciting challenge".

In conversation with Tommy Browne

D'Unbelievables

It was a Saturday evening in the summer of 1991, at the mart in Kilmallock. Jon Kenny and Pat Shortt were about to perform their new show, *One Hell Of A Do,* to a mixed audience of all ages, hungry and impatient to be entertained. As the very pungent odour of cattle dung wafted through the air, it seemed impossible to stage a creditable act in such circumstances. But not for Jon and Pat.

They might as well have been at the Royal Albert Hall. As the show unfolded the quintessential Irish rural wedding - the Galtee Regal Hotel was reenacted in all its would-be splendour, teeming with eminently recognisable characters. The frantic pace, the hilarious costumes, the spot-on characterisation pointed to caricature, the satire and wit and sheer talent brought the house down.

More than five years later, they are the most successful comedy duo in the country. The venues too are slightly more exalted - the Olympia, Tivoli and Andrews Lane theatres in Dublin, the Cork Opera House, Limerick's Belltable Arts Centre and University Concert Hall, the Tricycle Theatre in London, the Irish Arts Centre in New York.

Both Jon and Pat are genuinely stunned by the scale of their success. Their evolution from small-time pub (and mart) theatre to big-time stage and screen performers has been marked by a series of accidents - sax player Pat started as sound and lights man for solo comedian Jon, their on and off stage banter gradually developing into the core of the show.

So what's the secret? They both agree they are perfect foils for one another. "When we are working on a new show, it is usually obvious to each of us who should play what character", says Pat. Jon points out that ironically, most of Pat's characters tend to be older and more laid back, while those he plays are usually frantic and energetic, this despite the fact that Jon, at 39, is ten years older than Pat.

"Jon is a more natural performer than I am", says Pat generously. "I really find it harder to slip into character without the help of costume and props, whereas he can do it effortlessly".

But Jon reckons this facility has come with age, training and experience, the latter ranging from being a musician with a Glam rock band in the 70s to mime, classical dance and straight theatre as well as a very successful stint as a solo comedian in the eighties.

With technology the way it is now - D'Unbelievables have an e-mail address and get huge amounts of fanmail via the Internet! Unbelievable. It kinda makes you nostalgic for the Kilmallock cowdung.

Another key to the duo's success, leading to their award as Entertainers of the Year, is their genuine friendship. Pat's wife, Caroline, and Jon's wife, Margy, were also friends when they both attended Limerick School of Art and Design.

Being their own bosses means Jon and Pat never feel trapped in the partnership. They make their own decisions regarding career moves, allowing each other to pursue individual interests and projects. Jon appeared in the Roddy Doyle film, *The Van* for instance, and accomplished musician Pat played sax on the Sawdoctors' latest album. Both have appeared in British award-winning sit-com, *Fr. Ted,* and they took a couple of months off last summer to star in *Angela Mooney Dies Again* with Mia Farrow.

Thurles-born Pat who now lives in Castleconnell, says he's an "honorary Limerickman, except when Tipperary is playing against Limerick in the hurling". Jon comes from Hospital and now lives in a 180-year-old cottage by scenic Lough Gur. Both agree Limerick is a wonderful base from which to conduct their careers - they have no intention of moving.

In conversation with Marian Malone

Bishop Edward Darling

Right Rev. Edward Flewett Darling, Bishop of the United Dioceses of Limerick, Ardfert, Aghadoe, Killaloe, Kilfenora, Clonfert, Kilmacduagh and Emly entered the ordained ministry, following in the footsteps of several generations before him.

Speaking in the peaceful surroundings of his North Circular Road home, Bishop Darling recalls that it was not really expected of him to pursue the profession of his ordained father, but that it came as no surprise to his parents when he eventually informed them of his decision.

"I grew up in a County Cork rectory", says the Bishop, "and in the atmosphere of church life, and so from a fairly young age I felt I had a calling to enter the ministry. Not only was my father an archdeacon, but my mother's father, William Edward Flewett, was the Bishop of Cork from 1933 to 1938. I really think, however, that it was singing in a church choir, rather than my 'clerical connection', that finally convinced me that I had a vocation. Indeed, I still have a great interest in music and enjoy listening to anything from classical to jazz whenever time allows".

When he was eighteen years old, the young Edward Flewett Darling went to Trinity College, Dublin to complete an arts degree and to study for ordination. One of his interests as an undergraduate was singing in the University of Dublin Choral Society where he met Patricia Mann, herself an undergraduate, who four and a half years later was to become his wife. Coincidentally, Patricia was the daughter of a rector, her father later becoming the Dean of Down.

Edward was ordained in Belfast Cathedral in 1956 and served for the next thirty years in parishes in Bangor, County Down and in Belfast City, where their five children were born, reared and educated.

By the time of his appointment as Bishop of Limerick and Killaloe in 1985 their family had grown up and had already begun to follow their own chosen careers; so the new bishop and his wife began the latest chapter in their life on their own in Limerick.

> **"I do think that compulsory celibacy limits one's freedom of choice. I am not saying for one moment that celibacy is wrong. On the contrary, it can be a very good thing if chosen freely; but I certainly believe that it should be optional. Some are called to celibacy just as others are called to marriage."**

Speaking about his wife, Bishop Darling is obviously proud and very happy: "She has always been and continues to be a tremendous support to me. She understands what is expected of one, especially as she was brought up in the same clerical atmosphere and background as I.

Carrying out all my duties takes up a vast amount of time. The diocese is very large, spanning eight counties - I often think I would need a helicopter rather than a car!

My primary duty, of course, is to be a pastor, with particular responsibility to my clergy and their families. No two days of any bishop are ever alike and the diary gets filled up very quickly".

Asked about the veritable battering which has recently been directed against the Roman Catholic Church, the bishop stressed that it saddens him to see any branch of the Christian Church suffer like this, as it hinders the effectiveness of its mission as a whole. When asked specifically for his opinion on whether or not priests should be allowed to marry, he answered, "If I didn't agree with the marriage of clergy, I wouldn't be married myself."

In conversation with Claire Connolly Doyle

Philip Danaher

Sport in general, and rugby in particular, have played a major role in the life of thirty-one-year old Philip Danaher. At early age, he showed a remarkable talent for Gaelic Football, and played for Kerry, in the minor grade, and Limerick, in a Munster senior-final. Badminton and soccer were other sporting pastimes enjoyed by the versatile Danaher, but it was the oval ball game he first graced with local club, Abbeyfeale, in the under-age grade that was to gain his full-time attention.

In a career that spanned twenty-plus seasons, the man from Garryowen captained club, province and country. It has also enabled him to travel to venues in Australia, New Zealand, South Africa, Canada, U.S.A., Italy, France, England, Scotland, Wales and Northern Ireland.

"There is no greater honour than pulling on the green jersey of Ireland and running on to the pitch at Lansdowne Road."

Educated at St. Munchin's College, he won a Munster Senior Schools cup medal in 1982. "Winning the cup was a marvellous occasion and one I will long remember. We defeated Presentation Brothers Cork by double scores. As it was only the second occasion St. Munchin's won the cup, it made victory all the sweeter," he recalled.

Philp got his first taste of international rugby in 1982 representing the Irish Schools against England and Wales at outhalf. Having finished his studies at the Corbally College and after a short period with Garryowen, Philip moved to Dublin to continue his education at the Kevin Street Technical College and lined out with the Lansdowne club for the following four years.

In November 1987, the rugby career of Philip Danaher went into overdrive when he was first selected for Munster in the centenary meeting with Leinster, played at Thomond Park. The championship was eventually shared with Ulster, but the impressive displays by the young man from Limerick were noted by the Irish selectors, and two months later Philip made his international debut against Scotland at Lansdowne Road.

His return to Garryowen was a big plus for the Dooradoyle club, whom he led to victory in the All-Ireland league in the 1991-1992 season. Danaher is a big supporter of the national competition that has been won on five successive occasions by Limerick clubs.

There have been many memorable moments in the sporting life of Philip Danaher. "Being invited to captain the Irish team to tour New Zealand in 1992 was a great personal honour."

Other occasions were helping Garryowen to two All-Ireland League titles, Munster's defeat of Australia and winning twenty-eight Irish caps in three positions, fullback, centre and wing, while also representing the Barbarians.

Despite having to announce his premature retirement this year due to injury, Philip Danaher will not be lost to the game. After his magnificent service as a player to club, province and country, he will have much to contribute in a coaching capacity with Garryowen. Retirement from the game will also allow him to channel more energy into expanding the peat export business he set up in 1993.

In conversation with Michael O'Flaherty

Philomena Delaney

Philomena Delaney enjoys working with her hands. Professionally she is a skilled dental hygienist whilst her mastery of culinary skills has earned her the title Calor Gas Housewife of the Year 1995-1996.

This gift with her hands comes directly from her family tradition in craftwork. Philomena's father is a boat builder, founder of the family-run Kinsale and Kilmacsimon Boatyard and her mother enjoyed being at the heart of a warm, lively household, where all eleven children found fun and freedom to express themselves.

On leaving school, Philomena decided to pursue a career as a dental hygienist, a course of study not available at that time in Ireland. She trained in London's Royal Dental Hospital and continued on to complete a certificate in teaching. It was in London that she met her husband, Maurice Delaney, who, like Philomena, is originally from Cork. Shortly after their marriage the couple returned to Ireland and settled down to domestic happiness in Limerick in 1987. Philomena's career as a dental hygienist had allowed her the privilege of working on a part-time basis, giving her the opportunity to spend time with her two daughters, Katie aged eight and Erin aged six.

The path to winning the Calor Gas Housewife of the Year began with a neighbour in Corbally nominating Philomena for the competition. "My friend needed a new cooker. This was the ideal opportunity as the first prize for the regional final was a gas cooker. I was intrigued by the idea of competing in a discipline which I really enjoy and am confident in. The competition consisted of cooking a meal for two and attending an interview" recalled Philomena,

The young Philomena went straight for the cooker and enjoyed experimenting. "Anything I made was gobbled up in seconds. I had plenty of opportunity to make a flop and get the criticism! Being a member of a large family has distinct advantages."

neither element of which would cause concern to this vivacious, energetic woman. "My outrageous dessert won the hearts of the judges" she laughed. "As I moved along the various stages of the competition I met many different personalities and celebrities. It was great fun, but the live television was nerve-racking". On April 3rd, 1995, the National Concert Hall Dublin hosted the national finals and Limerick's Philomena Delaney was crowned winner.

The prize money of two thousand pounds was to be given to the charity of the winner's choice and Philomena chose Limerick-based Children at Risk Ireland (CARI), the support group for abused children.

Since winning the title, Philomena has been kept busy hosting cookery demonstrations throughout the country. "Most of the demonstrations are organised by Calor Gas on behalf of charities including Adapt House, Alzheimer's, Red Cross, the Irish Kidney Association and the Peto fund", said Philomena. "But you can't just stand up and fry for an audience! It's like a performance, you must entertain them".

Although not born or raised in Limerick, Philomena and Maurice Delaney have settled into Limerick life both professionally and domestically and agree "It is a beautiful place to live. Limerick has really changed and moved with the times. It's evident everywhere in the city".

Philomena's dream for her future is to add to the educational reputation of Limerick. "I would love to run a cookery school, imparting knowledge to young children in Limerick, which would encourage them to develop their skills and nurture their talent".

In conversation with Linda Lane

Teresa Delaney

The face of Teresa Delaney would not be instantly recognisable to most Limerick people, despite the fact that she has contributed enormously to helping the poor of the city for many years. While she herself would be embarrassed with the title, in many ways this Galway-born mother of five is Limerick's Mother Teresa.

For the past thirteen years, Teresa has worked on the Redemptorists' Christmas Food Appeal with Fr. Gerry Daly. Last Christmas this group helped organise and deliver 7,400 food parcels to the poor of Limerick, parcels valued at sixty pounds and more each.

"I have been going to the Novena at the Redemptorists since 1960 on Saturday evenings" explained Teresa, in answer to how she got involved with the "Reds" as the order at Mount Saint Alphonsus is affectionately known. "Fr. Daly came up to me about twelve years ago and asked me if I would like to help out and I have got great satisfaction from it every since," she explained.

This was shortly after the death of her husband John, who worked as a coach driver with CIE tours.

"I am a native of Corrandulla, County Galway. I came to Limerick in 1956 and began working with the Civil Service in Shannon. I met John, who was then driving the Shannon bus, and we started going out," she explained. The romance blossomed and John, who was from Sexton Street, married his Galway rose.

"Limerick has been very good to me. I have been blessed with the way I settled in and the many good friends I have made. They were invaluable to me when John passed away."

They had five children; Virginia O'Neill who teaches in Limerick; Catherine, the former Limerick Rose of Tralee in 1985, who is now married and living in California; Gerard who is living at home; Mary, a former member of the Irish Youth Orchestra, who is married and living in Boston; and Joseph who is also living at home with his mother.

Teresa is one of a family of four. Her late parents, Mary and Patrick Tyrrell, were what she terms "salt of the earth". They gave her a good Catholic upbringing, which has stood to her down through the years.

Along with Fr Daly, "she is everything from PRO to secretary of the Poor Campaign". The work is not only carried out at Christmas, but the whole year round.

Three years ago Teresa was honoured when she was asked to become the first female chief steward of the Annual Novena at Mount Saint Alphonsus, an event that attracts over 35,000 people each day of its duration.

Obviously Teresa's faith is very important to her, and she is a very strong believer in prayer.

While many find it difficult to have time to help others, Teresa Delaney stands out as a shining example of the work done quietly behind the scenes by many fine and caring people in Limerick.

In conversation with Eugene Phelan

Al Finucane

When Al Finucane's name is mentioned in local circles it is usually followed by the words 'modest', 'sportsman', 'gentleman', multi-talented and honour-laden. All these accolades rest lightly on his shoulders.

Born into one of Limerick's greatest sporting families, his grandfather Fonnie Neilan, captained Young Munsters to win the coveted Bateman Cup (All Ireland Champions) and Munster Senior Cup in 1928. His uncles John, "Batey", Christy and Gussie all played League of Ireland soccer with Limerick in the 1940s and 50s and they were instrumental, along with his mother Mary (Neilan) and father Paddy, in moulding the career of the young Alphonsus.

The first of Al's representative honours came when he was capped by the Republic of Ireland at Amateur level and he made his debut for the League of Ireland side against the Irish League in May, 1965. He was later to captain the side many times, and was honoured more than twenty-five times by the League. On the 5th of June, 1966, he played in Ireland's first U23 International in a 0-0 draw with France, and in 1967 he had a great innings in the full International side with an outstanding game in his first match against Turkey in Ankara. He went on to win a further ten caps against Czechoslovakia, Italy, Poland, Austria, Denmark, Hungary, Scotland. He captained the team against Austria.

Limerick won the Dublin City Cup in 1971 in a replayed win over Waterford with Al as skipper. Again that season Limerick were to savour their greatest hour in football with a victory over Drogheda United to win the F.A.I. Senior Cup. The following season, Al parted company with

Limerick to near neighbours Waterford with whom he enjoyed outstanding success.

An employee with Crescent Clothes - a highly successful gents' outfitters in the city - for many years, Al Finucane is now a manager at the Estuary Fuel Company in Limerick.

From the day he laced his first football boots to the first senior goal he scored in Flower Lodge in a career that spanned forty years he was still playing with local side Wembley Rovers up to last season.

He is also mindful of less fortunate members of society. "Since the beginning of time, sportspeople and high achievers have always been feted and admired, and probably always will be. But what about the ordinary man or woman, who rears a family on meagre earnings, or those who have beaten poverty, alcoholism or depression; much tougher opponents than Carl Lewis, Real Madrid or the All Blacks. These are the real champions and heroes!"

He played against the top sides in European Competition - the Champions Cup, the Cup Winners Cup and the UEFA or Fairs Cup. CSKA of Bulgaria, Torino of Italy, Hibernian F.C., Malta, Girondins Bordeaux F.C., France, AZ 67 Alkmaar, Holland. During his career he competed with World stars like Bobby Moore, Billy Bremner, Johnny Giles, Bobby Charlton, Patrick Battison and Albert of Hungary to mention a few.

The highlight of his long career occurred in 1967 when he was honoured by the Soccerwriters' Association of Ireland with the "Personality of the Year Award".

> **Al recalls meeting the Benefica team once at an airport en route back from Europe.**
> **"Their players asked us to swap club badges. We, of course, did not have any. That famous Limerick character, Mick Crowe, swapped with the illustrious Eusabio, revealing only later that he had in fact used his pioneer pin!"**

In conversation with Leonard Burke

Sr. Agnes Fitzgerald

Sr. Agnes Fitzgerald has had what might best be described as an on-off relationship with Limerick for most of her sixty-two years.

She has been director at the Cuan Mhuire Treatment Centre in Bruree for the past fourteen years, but her relationship with the county began when she was a child.

"I was about eight years of age before I really realised, in which county I lived. Our home at Cloughvoula was literally on the Cork, Kerry and Limerick border. We were in the county of Cork, the Diocese of Kerry, both my parents were from Kerry, our nearest town was Abbeyfeale in County Limerick and I went to Mass in Mountcollins, County Limerick. My association with Limerick was strengthened when I went to 'Miss Woulfe's' school, as it was fondly known, in Abbeyfeale".

However that association with the county was to be severed for thirty years when she entered the Mercy Convent in Ardee, County Louth, aged eighteen.

"I taught for many years at our primary school in Ardee, but my sister, Sr. Consillio, who runs the Cuan Mhuire Treatment Centre at Athy, had asked me to give just one year to the work of Cuan Mhuire. The centre was newly opened and, in the days before I came, I felt that I was being asked to make the biggest sacrifice of my life, but once here I felt totally at home with the people and the work".

Referring to her work with the residents of Cuan Mhuire, Sr. Agnes believes that addiction cannot be seen in isolation - we must see the whole person - the person created to the Image and Likeness of God Himself.

"There is no such thing as a hopeless case."

People from all walks of life come to Cuan Mhuire for help. There, they are made feel at home and introduced to the Cuan Mhuire programme, which includes detoxification where necessary, followed by a thirty-five-day intensive course, which includes individual and group conselling.

"Addiction is no respecter of class, race, creed or background. If a person is very far gone drinking alcohol or using drugs for many years, they have usually lost their families, their homes, their jobs, their health and whatever money they may have had. But a common loss among most of the people I have come across during the years is that of their own self respect and sense of responsibility".

"We should never forget that they are wonderful people suffering from an illness. Once they begin to see their own goodness, giftedness and capacity to recover, it is amazing how quickly people get well".

She made a very interesting discovery when she researched the history of the house and the buildings at Cuan Mhuire.

"It was originally owned by a landlord named Fethersonhaugh, who went bankrupt around the time of the famine. After his death, his wife and one of his two sons emigrated to Australia. His second son was then in college in England. Twice his mother sent him the fare to Australia, twice he gambled it."

Sr. Agnes sees it as no mere coincidence that a house that is so involved in addiction today should have such a history.

In conversation with Cathy Halloran

Desmond FitzGerald

Desmond FitzGerald is the 29th Knight of Glin, in an unbroken chain of dynastic life which stretches from the early fourteenth century. He is the proprietor of Glin Castle, a "pasteboard Gothic house" which has "pastry-crust crenellations".

While Glin Castle has been the family seat since the 1790's, the future looks dodgy for this great Munster family, as the Knight is the first to tell you that he has three adult daughters, who are living their own lives. However, despite being an avid and thoroughly schooled historian (MA from Harvard Fogg Art Museum) and canny businessman, Desmond FitzGerald conveys a benign optimism when musing with the question, what next with Glin Castle, if he be the final Knight.

He sees it as part of his inheritance to educate people as to the value of their ascendancy heritage, houses and art and to generate the means to make living, commercial properties of those surviving.

A keen sense of realism is spliced by his gift as a ferocious mimic, and his interests at every level keep him sharp as the lance his ancestors bore.

The 500-acre demesne has a productive dairy farm which supplies milk to Dawn Dairies. Glin Castle also offers country estate accommodation of the finest order behind its perfect walls. Business is good, with American businessmen topping the guest list for secluded, antiquated luxury.

"We have had an interesting array of people here over the years," the Knight ("call me Knight") recalls with some satisfaction. "Mick Jagger has been and gone and President Lyndon Johnson's wife, Ladybird Johnson, was another. But privacy is a big factor in why a VIP would choose to stay at Glin and not in one of the bigger castles, so I can't tell you about others."

Desmond FitzGerald is a Renaissance man, rooted in the daily concerns of running a profitable business, of establishing a degree course in Art History at the University of Limerick, of chivvying the government into investing in our great buildings, of being an agent for Christy's Auctioneers and of being a committed author and publisher.

"Houses and castles such as Glin cannot be kept by mummified dodos living in a solitary, lunatic fashion."

With Professor Anne Crookshank of Trinity College, he has published various impressive tomes and is currently writing a book on Irish furniture. His wife, Olda FitzGerald, is an endearing hostess and commendable writer herself.

The Knight of Glin is one of three old families still living in their Munster houses of yore:

"There is Bantry, there is Mount Ievers and there is us.'Us' is the Glin branch known as the Black Knight or the Knight of the Valley. There has been a White Knight and a Knight of Kerry, other cadet branches of the FitzGerald's, Earls of Desmond."

Blissful is the life in this manor here on the southern bank of the Shannon River. The Knight of Glin and his guests can enjoy the perfect aspect in comfort. Perhaps his best legacy will be the history and restoration work he does locally with FÁS projects and in challenging the nation's dozy conscience where its architectural gems are concerned.

In conversation with Rose Rushe

Mary and Dick Fitzgerald

Mary Ryan was up to her neck in voluntary work as secretary of her local Macra branch in Ballyneety when Dick was her blind date escort to the annual dinner dance. They were engaged for Mary's twenty-first birthday on December 4th 1972 and the following August the receptionist at Steve Foley's Shannon Arms Hotel in Limerick City married Castleisland-born Dick, who was farming in Adare.

The Fitzgeralds were supplying soft fruit to multiples and the catering trade and growing Brussels sprouts. "It was the first winter when I was packing sprouts and the house was full of the smell of them that I told Dick there had to be easier ways of making money", Mary recalls.

When he built his farmhouse in Adare, Dick Fitzgerald fitted each bedroom with washbasins - "something unheard of then in a family home" says Mary. The Fitzgerald success saga started in August 1976 when the family opened up three bedrooms to guests. Dick cooked the breakfasts and did the wash-up, Mary's mother Helen provided the homemade bread, and Mary did the serving. By the end of that first season they were planning expansion, and four extra rooms had been added on before the arrival of daughter Elaine the following May.

A 1979 trip to the USA for Mary and Dick turned into an ideas-gathering mission. They were especially impressed by the combination of budget prices and full facilities at the Day's Inns hotels and decided that something similar would work in Adare.

> **"Put enough on the plate the first time, and they'll always come back."**
> **Mary Fitzgerald**

The 1980s had been good to the Fitzgeralds and West Limerick with the construction phase of the Aughinish Alumina plant adding year-round demand to tourist business. In the meantime the ever-ready-to-please policy of the Fitzgeralds meant they were providing more and more evening meals, catering for parties and then for weddings.

Their youngest child, Richard, arrived in May 1982 and the following year the twelve American-style rooms became the nucleus of the Woodlands House Hotel, which opened on July 16th.

The hotel has been growing ever since, but keeping the "feel at home" natural warmth of a closely-knit family environment. "Our hotel gives rural people a chance to come here and feel comfortable in the type of surroundings which they would not normally visit. We have carved out our own family market," says Mary.

Dick and Mary plunged into a £1.8 million expansion in 1991, which brought the number of rooms up to thirty-two, adding on a conference room and cocktail bar and the impressive hotel lobby. "We didn't skimp and it paid off handsomely," says Mary.

Although grown to fifty rooms, eighty full-time and forty part-time staff, the family character of Woodlands House Hotel is growing too. Mary's seventy-one year-old mother is still putting the bread on the table and Mary and Dick have been joined by son David on the management team, with Elaine ready to follow after studies at the Shannon College of Hotel Management.

In conversation with Dermot Walsh

—50—

John Fitzgerald

GETTING to the top in your chosen sport and honoured to represent your country, while also being successful in business, is a goal aspired to by many but not always attained, particularly in rugby football.

For John Fitzgerald, a sales executive with Lombard and Ulster Bank, success with the oval ball was always evident from a young age, and would eventually yield twelve full Irish caps. He also made five "appearances" and captained the Irish 'B' side, represented the Combined Provinces, Barbarians and the English selected side, Penguins.

John, who was born in London thirty-five years ago, returned to Ireland a few years later.

His conversion to the sport he would grace at the highest level came at school, where his height and frame was ideal for the prop forward position. "I played rugby in St. Munchin's College on the junior team, but missed the cup campaign due to injury", he recalled.

"What makes Limerick the rugby capital of Ireland is the determination and pride the players have in their city and clubs."

John's first rugby success was with Young Munsters as a member of the the Under-16 league and cup winning teams. Not surprisingly, the exceptional talent of the young Fitzgerald was quickly noted, and he made his initial appearance in the Munster Senior Cup three years later to be followed by selection on the Munster team.

On January 16th, 1988 he achieved his sporting ambition when he played for Ireland against Scotland at Lansdowne Road. "It was an occasion I will never forget. Philip Danaher also made his debut on that day and with Willie Sexton on the team, there was a big Limerick interest in the match that Ireland won on a 22-18 scoreline."

Having played senior rugby for seventeen seasons, John, with brothers Michael and Edward , is also involved in the family business running the popular Corner Flag Bar in Henry Street. "The pub scene coupled with the sporting life generates a great buzz in the city."

He is also quick to discount the adverse publicity heaped on Limerick. "If the people in the media spent only half the time here as it takes them to write their derogatory stories, they might learn the true facts. Every city has its problems, but there is much more good than bad here and I will always do everything in my power to promote Limerck at every opportunity."

John points to the success of local rugby as determination and pride in club and city which makes an "unbeatable combination". Rugby has changed dramatically since it went fully professional in August 1995, and it is a worrying trend. "It will be difficult to financially support four clubs in Division One of the All-Ireland League. Perhaps in the near future we will have just a Limerick team to compete against the best club sides in the world. The national league will probably continue, but it will have a lesser role."

John has many happy memories from his involvement in rugby that include winning his first Irish cap, playing in the World Cup and being a member of the Young Munsters team that won the All-Ireland League in 1993. Honoured with the captaincy of the Young Munsters club during the '95/'96 season, their centenary year, he looks forward to the new season with the same enthusiasm he displayed in the past.

In conversation with Michael O'Flaherty

—52—

Paddy Glynn

For most of his life, solicitor Patrick Anthony Glynn lived in the splendid elegance of the Crescent, just around the corner from the family shop in Hartstonge Street.

Acting and debating were two of his main interests but he also played rugby and competed in the Munster Schools Junior Cup.

"To this day I don't know if it was reading the papers or listening to Perry Mason on the radio, but I decided I wanted to be a lawyer so I got apprenticed to the late James Sexton and qualified in 1956."

Paddy Glynn's natural confidence, coupled with stylish pin-striped suits, capped by buttonhole roses gave him a man about town image. He took part in a few shows with the Cecilians and also served as secretary and president of the Old Crescent Rugby Club. He was the quintessential Limerickman. At one stage he was even dubbed Limerick's most eligible bachelor by a female journalist.

"If people from the Provinces do not make the sacrifice, you will find that every President of the Law Society is going to come from the capital city, even though half the profession live outside the Pale."

His chairmanship of Tuairim, an organisation for public debate on social issues in pre-television days, brought a touch of liberal thinking to a city still emerging from post war isolation.

"There was a vacancy for a local representative of the profession on the Law Society. I ran and was elected and once I became involved I did not have much time for other interests," he said. "I spent about seventeen years on the Council and I was elected President of the Law Society in 1995."

From an ambitious school boy in the fifties, Paddy Glynn rose to head the Law Society in the nineties. In that time one of the great changes he has seen is the sheer number of solicitors coupled with the entry of many young women into the profession.

"Over fifty percent of the profession are women and over fifty percent are under thirty-five. In the profession there has never been any problem with women; they are colleagues," he says.

From the cosy consensus of the Fifties, the legal profession has now changed radically and the next decade shall present daunting new challenges.

"The problem of confidentiality, which is very important in a solicitor's life, is a matter for the future," he said. "More and more we are faced with conflicts like tax evasion, drug profits and money laundering.

On the one hand, you can't be seen to support organised crime, yet if a man says he wants to buy a house for cash, do you rush off to inform the Government?"

"Somebody has to defend people on drug charges. If you defend them are they entitled to confidentiality? Are alleged drug dealers entitled to legal representation? Are they to be denied Constitutional rights?"

Paddy Glynn poses the questions stopping for a few seconds to consider each one. It is a whole world away from a crackling radio and a young schoolboy listening to Perry Mason.

In conversation with Frank Hamilton

Michael and Joan Griffin

In the Griffin household it is definitely a case of ladies first - Joan generally finishes ahead of her husband Michael when they compete in triathlons.

But that is no surprise really - she is one of the countries best competitors, regularly finishing near the top of the field in events at home and abroad.

Now competing as a master, the forty-one year old athlete finished fifth in the European Championships in 1996, and hopes in 1997 to go at least two places better. The difference between her and the bronze medal was just three minutes, so there will be no let-up in training over the winter.

The couple, living in Monaleen, have carved out a successful life for themselves since coming to Limerick in 1977. Michael, a general practitioner and a sports medicine specialist, is a native - "a fifth-generation undertaker," he joked.

His father died when he was just five, and he feels that this made him independent and self-reliant. "People kept telling me he was a very handsome man - then they'd say, I don't look a bit like him," laughed the doctor.

They met as students in UCC - on St Patrick's night in 1972. Joan was a first year arts student, studying Archeology, English and Sociology. Michael was a fourth year medical student. Two years later they got married.

Their early years were spent in Drogheda, but in 1977 they settled in Limerick. Michael now runs a very successful practice in St John's Square. Since 1985 he has been involved, through UCC, in training GPs. Three years ago he was instrumental in setting up a scheme in Limerick for training new general practitioners at the University of Limerick.

In addition Dr Griffin has recently completed a master's degree in sports medicine.

Although when they met first the couple were into "music and *craic*", sport soon became an important part of their lives. It began when they entered a superstars competition in the Hurlers' Pub. They followed this with the initial Dublin City Marathon, in 1980. Michael has not missed a Dublin City Marathon since, though Joan has missed some, due to injuries, and to having had four daughters - Ciara (21), Laoise (19), Murna (17), and Shona (14).

> "I am a professional, but what I earn would not buy a dinner. I remember once winning a series of three races, and getting £15. It cost me £5 to enter each race!"
>
> **Joan Griffin**

When the triathlon craze first hit the country the two were to the forefront - Michael as an administrator and Joan as one of the country's leading competitors.

The triathlon is a gruelling event. The short-course race involves a swim of just under a mile, a forty kilometre cycle, and a ten kilometre run. The long-course event (or half-ironman) involves a swim of a mile and a quarter, a cycle of fifty-six miles, and a run of thirteen miles.

Joan has been seven times an Irish international, and still competes as fiercely as ever. Professionalism has entered the sport, though the money involved does not match tennis, boxing or soccer.

Both agree that the triathlon has given them the opportunity to travel, meet new people, and have great *craic*. "It is good that we have a hobby that we can both do together," said Michael.

In conversation with Tom Healy

Helen Gannon

One of Helen Gannon's most treasured and enduring memories goes back to her childhood - when as a tender six-year-old she was brought for her first Irish dancing lessons to Mrs. Le Gear.

After graduating as a registered nurse and midwife from the Regional Hospital, Galway, she emigrated from her native "Parish" area of Limerick in 1967 with husband, PJ. A native of Dunmore, Co. Galway, he later became Professor of Psychiatry at St. Louis University, Missouri.

She found the initial task of adjusting to America immensely difficult - even settling in to their new home was a burden.

"Our very first house was lovely but we didn't know where to sit because in Ireland you sit facing the fire! Everyone said: 'You sit facing the television!' So finally they put a TV in the middle of the room and I sat in front of it. Everyone was happy - except me. I was miserable. All I could think of was how long it would take to make enough money to get back home".

Happily, the family had an accordion, Helen says now with a smile, "before we had a dining room table" and that gave them the impetus to play Irish music, dance and talk to one another.

And it was to become a source of true inspiration for her and her family - sons Seán, now 31, Niall, 28, Liam, 27 and Eileen, 19.

Helen's view is that Irish culture is so rare and so beautiful that it deserves the best possible setting,

"Every nation should cherish its own culture and identity, its language, its music, song and dance. We should never back away from taking pride in our past and becoming swamped in cultural trends that may be alien to us."

one which will enhance the image of Ireland and its people everywhere.

As PRO for Comhaltas Ceoltóirí Éireann in North America, she directs major and highly successful programmes and workshops in her adopted city of St. Louis and the entire United States covering a whole spectrum of our culture, including Irish dance, instrumental and voice training.

Helen keeps in close contact with her family - her wonderful and vibrant Mum, Sadie Phillips, as well as her close-knit siblings, Gerard, Cyril, and Ann.

Her American family is steeped in Irish music - between them they have won many highly-cherished awards including world championships. Harpist daughter Eileen recalls that she started step-dancing "as soon as I could walk".

Remembering back to her early days in Limerick, Helen fondly recalls "We had to perform for everyone who walked in the door. Every time we had visitors it was the done thing to end it with a little performance of some description. My sister and mother played the piano, my brother the accordion - and I danced."

If Helen has any concerns about the advance of Irish music, which she and her family love so dearly, it is the lack of any apparent formal structure to train musicians.

Helen and PJ have lived abroad for over thirty years - but it has not dimmed their love of homeland. Ireland lives powerfully in a corner of their hearts.

In conversation with Noel Smith

Michael Guerin

Shannon will be central to future aviation developments, predicts Michael Guerin, the former general manager who steered the airport, through some of the most critical years of its history.

Now retired after being at the helm in Shannon for seven years, Michael Guerin is quite confident that when the new giants of the skies, aircraft with the capacity to carry 800 passengers, come into operation, Shannon will still be the Crossroads of the World.

Apart from his early years in Templemore and later in Limerick, where he lives off the Ennis Road, Michael, has strong links with County Clare. His father, a garda, was born in Quin and his mother, in Kilkishen. He was the eldest of five children and after leaving school, he entered the public service through the Department of Post and Telegraphs. In the mid 60s Michael transferred to the Department of Transport and shortly afterwards he was assigned to Shannon, just before Aer Rianta, took over the management of the three airports, - Dublin, Shannon and Cork, in 1969.

However, Michael says there were dark clouds still on the horizon. "The troubles in the North of Ireland had a negative effect on tourism, particularly from the North American market."

He also lists the hike in fuel prices in the 1970s as badly affecting transit traffic through the airport.

"Tourism is the main growth industry of the future and hand-in-hand with that will go aviation."

Michael Guerin, explains that it was mainly out of these crises that one of the most innovative ideas with far-reaching developments emerged. He conceived the idea of Aer Rianta offering to construct for Aeroflot a completely new aviation fuel farm with related facilities at Shannon.

Reflecting on this project, Michael adds that one of the first associated developments was the establishment of Shannon Aviation Fuels, which enabled Aer Rianta to sell Soviet fuel and later western fuels to other airlines. He is happy too that it was this relationship built up at Shannon between Aeroflot and Aer Rianta that was instrumental in the successful negotiations of a joint venture with the Russian airlines in 1987, to set-up the duty-free shop in Moscow Airport.

Michael, of course, was the first general manager of Aer Rianta International, before being appointed general manager, Shannon, in 1989.

He was also responsible for the innovation that led to U.S. Pre-Immigration Clearance and recalls that he had spent over eight years working with its Washington-based headquarters before the first such centre was opened in Shannon in 1986.

He was awarded the coveted Innovator of the Year Award for his contribution to the Aeroflot development and the establishment of U.S. Pre-Clearance, the only person to date to have received the award twice.

In 1995, Michael was also honoured by the Limerick Chamber of Commerce by being elected President that year.

On the future he's optimistic. He says: "The change in Shannon's transatlantic status had some adverse effects on traffic." He is confident however, that the future growth of tourism will lift all airports and Shannon, he predicts, will quickly bounce back to its former place in world travel.

In conversation with Tommy Browne

Lord and Lady Harrington

The Right Honourable Earl of Harrington has made Limerick his home for the past fifty years. With his wife, the Countess of Harrington, an active but tranquil life is enjoyed by them in their new home in Ballingarry, County Limerick. They met at a dinner party in Limerick and have had a lifetime of involvement with horses, fishing, shooting and many related businesses.

Lord Harrington, who insists that his friends call him 'Bill', left school at seventeen years of age, to join the army and later for a life in the horse business. His fondest memory of the early years include the winning of the Maiden Plate with *Revelry,* whom he sold on to win the Irish National. It's difficult to imagine this tall, formidable gentleman as an eleven-and-a-half stone jockey, but in 1947, shortly after arriving to Ireland, Lord Harrington competed as such. He began his first stud business at Dooneen in Patrickswell. In spite of the move from their beloved home of thirty years at Greenmount in Patrickswell, the wedding of their daughter Isabella "consummated the Balllingarry house as a home." This event was especially important for the Countess, whose love of the South-West encouraged her to choose a move to Ballingarry.

"Why would we consider living anywhere else? Limerick is a beautiful place which has provided us with much happiness over the thirty-two years of our married life."
Lady Harrington

Lord Harrington is passionate in his commitment to make the horse business in Limerick an international success. Having led the Limerick Hunt as Master and Fieldmaster intermittently since the 1950s, he is also associated with several other groups and societies in Limerick. With the help of the Castletown committee, the Irish Olympic Horse Society was established under his chairmanship. From the outcome of meetings often held at the Harringtons' former Patrickswell home, funds were raised to send the first three-day event team to the Olympics in Rome and the first major international three-day event in Ireland was organised for Punchestown.

Lord Harrington is well noted for his powers of persuasion, and the Department of Finance have been witness to this on many occasions. "I'm a bit of a rebel when it comes to getting my own way sometimes", he explained, as he recalled the lifting of restrictions on Irish bloodstock. The influence of Lord Harrington prompted the Department of Finance to change the tax laws so as to allow partnerships in ownership of stallions to benefit financially in the same way as private owners.

The Game and Country Fair was established at Adare eighteen years ago, but the location has now changed to Clonshire. The majority of the proceeds are donated to local charities. This Clonshire Centre was established by the Harringtons with the purpose of bringing together all sectors of the adjoining communities. The centre boasts excellent facilities, which include horseriding lessons, showjumping and football, and stages many agricultural events. The Harringtons consider their careers and social lives to be intermingled and are driven by their concern that "much more has to be done in the direction of hunting, shooting, fishing, coursing, and all other field sports".

The Harringtons are determined to further the reputation of Irish bloodstock internationally. They are certain that Limerick will be the centre for equestrian development and are proud of their association with it.

In conversation with Linda Lane

Gerard Hartmann

Talking to Gerard Hartmann, physiotherapist to the 1996 Irish Olympic team, is probably as close as you could get to undergoing an invigorating massage on your attitude. The result: a refreshing, tingling sensation across your whole outlook, and the reassurance that success or failure in life is largely determined by your mental approach.

"I never wake up to a dark day. Every day brings some new challenge and reward", says the leading international sports injury therapist. Now resident in Florida, Gerard's daily routine brings him in contact with international athletes and sportspeople, who come from around the globe to benefit from his highly acclaimed skills and techniques. A career that began only seven years ago, Gerard's reputation has earned him the respect and custom of leading names in the world of athletics. These include top Irish athletes, such as Sonia O'Sullivan, Marcus O'Sullivan and Catherina McKiernan, as well as a plethora of other international stars. Among these are Kenyan Moses Kiptanui, steeplechase world record holder, Douglas Wakiihuri, the 1990 New York City Marathon winner and Russia's Valentina Egorova, the 1992 Olympic marathon champion. The list goes on ...

"The funny thing about it is that it literally happened by accident!", says Gerard. In his earlier years, he had different career plans. After working for a short time in the family jewellery business, he went to make his mark in the international athletics scene. Becoming Irish triathlon champion seven times saw at least some dreams of being a sporting legend come through, but it wasn't meant to be. A cycling accident in 1991 put an end to competitive athletics for Gerard, and marked a major turning point in his life.

"As I lay on my hospital bed, I made a decision to channel the energy that I had previously put into the triathlons into my career as a sports injury therapist. I really believe that with enthusiasm and determination, anything is possible." The rest is history.

Reminiscing on highlights in his career to date, Gerard refers immediately to the 1996 Olympics. "It was a great honour to be the first Limerickman to be on an Irish Olympic medical team. It was a wonderful experience, especially being part of the high that Michelle Smith's wins brought about."

So what is the secret of his success? One athlete and patient summarised it as "a rare combination of qualities that inspire trust." Gerard himself believes that it has to do with really understanding what the athletes are going through; something that is only possible by having participated in competitive athletics. Confidence and a will to succeed are also key factors. "I get as much of a thrill out of curing a patient as I would have from winning a race a few years back!"

Looking ahead, Gerard has no doubt about where he is going in the future. His ancestors, watchmakers by trade, came to Limerick from Germany in 1877, and stayed. "I don't intend to break that tradition. Although I have built my career abroad, Limerick is where my heart is." With his reputation now well established, Gerard is intent on setting up his main clinic in Limerick during 1997, attracted not only by the impressive sports and training facilities of the city, but also, and especially, by the quality of life.

> "I look forward very much to bringing some of the world's top athletes to my home city, and in this way giving back something to the place and people that have inspired me all my life."

In conversation with Mary Fennelly

Una Heaton

Una Heaton and her five brothers and three sisters grew up in Rathbane and, with one exception, still live in the Limerick area. Her mother, a native of Dublin, moved to Kilrush at a young age and there she met and fell in love with Joe Lynch, a well-known Limerick bookie. Smiling fondly, Una recalls, "my mother was instantly smitten". Joe passed away last year, but some of his traits obviously live on in this bubbly, outgoing and vivacious woman. And her mother's love of art has obviously rubbed off too.

Una went to school at the Presentation Convent in Limerick and subsequently studied at the College of Art and Design in the late sixties. Instead of pursuing a career as a teacher, she decided to set up her own art business - the first studio in a basement on O'Connell Street. "Things went well and I decided to move up the street, and up in the world a bit, to a new studio". Later on, secure in the knowledge that a colleague was in charge of her studio, she went to Amsterdam in 1969 with the intention of spending a working summer there. Two years later she was still in Holland working in a hotel. "It was a very big and quite prestigious hotel and I was, subsequently, invited by the management to redesign the hotel's image, as appropriate. On completion of my assignment, I was delighted to have been offered the job of resident artist. This, in turn, has influenced my career at home in Dromoland Castle and Jurys' Hotels, where I specialised in signage, portraiture and drawing caricatures of the guests." She has also prepared various decorative themes for special occasions.

> **"Alongside my preference for character work, scenery takes second place. I think the face tells a lot and I'm fascinated by some of the characters I come across along the west coast."**

Home for Una and John Heaton and their two teenage children, Emma and Barry, is Limerick's North Circular Road. A prominent figure in Garryowen RFC, John captained the club to Munster Junior Cup victory some years ago. Born in Athlone, he established a clothing industry in Hartstonge Street, but later moved into the catering business in Moscow by opening a Chinese Restaurant. Una is a keen follower of rugby and frequents as many matches as possible.

These days Una works from home. She has had a number of very successful exhibitions in locations as varied as the Aran Islands and the Shankill Road in Belfast.

At the launch of the Aran Islands' exhibition she met one old local chap nursing a glass of wine. Striking up a conversation, Una asked him if he liked to drink wine. "Only at exhibitions" was the reply.

Una likes to turn her hand to all sorts of projects, one of which is organising *Murder Mystery Weekends* for corporate clients. She's also very actively committed to the Peace Movement and designed the much-worn peace badge, incorporating the white ribbon symbol. "I really feel I want to work for peace - to help make people realise that we can live together and don't have to kill another person to get our views across. Cross-border understanding and co-operation are vital components in our peace-building activities. I'm an optimistic person, and take a positive view of the future."

In conversation with Kieran McConville

Paul Hogan

There are very few cities in the world that have a breed of pigeon named after them. Limerick is one of these, home to the Limerick Short-Faced Tumbler. Bred over the past thirty years, the man responsible for spreading the fame and the name of 'Limerick' throughout the feathered world, is Limerick man, Paul Hogan.

Born in 1963, Paul Hogan grew up 'slap bang in the middle' of his six brothers and five sisters in their Garryowen family home.

The Limerick Short Faced Tumbler was originally bred by the late Michael MacDonald from Garryowen, who brought back two 'short-faced' clean legged, tumblers, from England in the late 1950s. While he appreciated their free-flying tumbling displays, Michael didn't like the way they trailed their tails and wings on the ground, and decided to cross breed them with a feather legged 'booted tumbler'. This cross-breeding took about fifteen years to mature and created a unique new strain of bird. The new breed almost died out, however, when Michael's loft was broken into, and most of his birds were taken, leaving him with only two pairs of Tumblers. He decided to give these to Austin Quinn from Thomondgate.

Paul Hogan first took an interest in pigeons when he was about eleven years of age. "Every Sunday we used to be sent up to the Redemptorist's – my six brothers and myself – to say the Rosary. Until one Sunday morning, when we heard on the radio that Ranks was to close". Paul explains that in hindsight they realised what was actually said was that Ranks would close 'in three to five years' but admits "we picked it up wrong at the time, thinking the mill was closing straight away". The seven Hogan brothers decided to skip their Sunday morning prayers that same day and climbed over St Clement's wall and Ranks wall and went up around the empty flour mills. They went right up through the deserted buildings and caught lots of pigeons and put them in empty flour sacks. "We thought we were saving them because the mill was being closed and we brought them home. After getting a hiding from both our parents for skipping prayers, my father finally cooled down and put a loft together for me from bread trays – and from then on I was hooked on pigeons."

The 'Limerick's' first official show was in Dublin during 1986 and Paul recalls the excitement of the other show entrants with the new breed.

"The *Limerick* is in the top five of the most sought after pigeons in the country and will remain on top for many years to come."

The Limerick Short-Faced Tumbler was officially recognised in 1994 when it was given a class of its own in the National Show. This year, judges from England were in attendance at the show in Dublin and reporting in *The Feathered World* they gave the breed their seal of approval.

Now that the 'Limerick' is on the Internet, countless pairs of the birds have been sent to England, Northern Ireland, Scotland, Wales, Europe, South Africa and Australia.

In conversation with Ron Kirwan

John Hunt, Junior

John Hunt, Junior was weaned on art, archaeology and history and spent most of his youth in the castles of Bunratty, Knappogue and Craggaunowen. "My earliest memories are of driving from Dublin to Bunratty where the family stayed until the castle was restored. We then moved into a caravan on the grounds of the folk park."

From there the Hunt family moved to Knappogue Castle and then onto Craggaunowen. Looking back, with great pride and enjoyment on those early years when his father, John Hunt, was restoring the heritage of the region, John Junior says: "I was never bored."

John Junior is the son of John and Gertrude Hunt, collectors of the priceless Hunt Collection, which has been donated to the Irish people. The Hunt family are rightly numbered amongst the most generous benefactors of this nation.

The art and archaeological items were collected with the specific intention of displaying them together to illustrate the progression of craftsmanship and the decorative art through the ages.

John Hunt, Junior and his sister Trudy have single-mindedly worked to achieve their parents' ambition to display the collection in Limerick. Despite adversities and many temptations to make life more agreeable by selling the collection, John Hunt, Junior gave up his job to make sure the collection was housed in one place in Limerick. His dream will come true when the Hunt Museum is officially opened in the Old Custom House in Limerick.

John Junior was educated in Glenstal Abbey. He is married to Patricia Mooney and they have three children. He has already a chequered career having worked for the Arts Council and the Temple Bar Gallery.

One of the strengths of the Hunt Collection is its wide-ranging content. The range covers objects commissioned and used by both ecclesiastical and legal patrons, and includes statues in stone, bronze and wood; crucifixes, panel paintings, metalwork, jewellery, enamels, ceramics and crystal; and an important collection of Irish archaeological artefacts from Neolithic flints, through Bronze Age gold, the unique eighth century Antrim Cross, hand-pins, brooches and penal crucifixes.

In 1991 and again in 1995 the Hunt family magnanimously presented other collections to the Nation, including works of Picasso and Gauguin, a bronze horse considered to be from the hand of Leonardo de Vinci, a Greek silver coin revered as one of the biblical "30 pieces of silver" and a personal seal of Charles I of England.

The Hunt Museum is scheduled to open in January 1997. John declared: "What will make the museum different is that most museums set out to educate in the old Victorian sense or they try to improve your mind or tell you a story - the Hunt Museum will be concerned primarily with the objects and in that sense the museum at the Custom House will reflect the type of atmosphere we had at our home. It will not be strictly chronological. You weave your way up and down through different periods, through different nationalities, so the emphasis is on encouraging interest or a sense of wonderment."

> "The museum will also have a 'touching room' because in our home we were permitted to physically touch the items in question."

In conversation with Eileen Brophy

Muirne Hurley

For the lovely Muirne Hurley, Limerick's winner of the 1994 Rose Of Tralee, her reign will be something she will never forget.

"I never realised there was so much involved in being the Rose Of Tralee, but I thoroughly enjoyed the challenge" says the affable, red-headed Muirne who was twenty-three when she captured the much sought-after Rose Of Tralee crown.

An accomplished musician, singer and harpist, she also has a degree in business studies, with languages, from Limerick University. She's at present employed as a sales executive with Tipperary Natural Mineral Water, covering the west and southwest region of Ireland from her home in Limerick.

The week of the Rose Of Tralee competition will stand out in Muirne's mind forever. All the contestants met in Dublin and after being introduced to the judges at various receptions there, they were off to Limerick. The most memorable highlight for Muirne was returning home along with the other Roses. The girls were given a civic reception and then a parade followed with the Roses being escorted up Limerick's O'Connell Street. The crowd's reaction was warm and friendly; people waving and cheering before the Roses made their journey on a bus to Tralee. "It was a great way to get to know the girls. You should have heard the din thirty-two of us made on that bus!"

"We all forgot about the competition. Lots of people think the judging is done on the night of the T.V. programme, but, in fact, it goes on all week".

Muirne admits to being sick with nerves the night of the T.V. broadcast from the Dome, with host Gay Byrne.

"Once I got on stage, I relaxed a little and when Gay unexpectedly called on Dad, Garda Cormac Hurley to sing, I completely forgot my nerves, because I knew Dad was taken completely by surprise. He sang *The Rose of Tralee* and somehow, I got through my solo, *Limerick, You're a Lady*. The relief I felt coming off that stage is indescribable".

When Muirne was announced as the winner of the competition, she admits to a complete blur in her mind.

> "During my year as Rose Of Tralee, I received such support, warmth, dedication and friendliness, that I actually felt humbled."

"Suddenly I was being kissed and hugged by the other girls. I looked down to where Mum and Dad were sitting, and saw Dad with tears pouring down his face. Mum was jumping up and down with excitement and my uncle, was running up and down the hall waving a banner!"

During Muirne's year of office, she attended hundreds of functions around Ireland and abroad. She appeared live on Australian T.V. and presented two *Shop Ireland* programmes on U.S. Coast to Coast Television. She was also a judge in the John Player *Tops Of The Town* competition.

Muirne's happy to be back in her native Limerick. "Limerick is an exciting place to live. The night life is great and I absolutely love the whole buzz of the city".

"The Limerick people are also fantastically generous when it comes to fund-raising for various charities. They really are the salt of the earth".

In conversation with Valerie Sweeney

Liam Irwin

He is a most unusual academic, a man who began work as a banker, returned to study as a mature student and now heads the history department of Mary Immaculate College of Education. A serious approach to heritage is softened by his admission that he occasionally watches a television soap opera.

In a way, the career path of Liam Irwin mirrors the expansion of Limerick and that of the college. When he joined the academic staff in 1977, it was expanding to degree institution status. Later, the greatest change was the link with the University of Limerick, which has now added an international dimension to the teaching work of the history department.

"We have more Arts students than B. Ed., but both are important to the college," he said in his book-lined study. "The link with UL and the BA students led to major changes. Even my own work, for example, involves having students study abroad."

In 1992, Liam Irwin went as a visiting professor to the University of Maryland and forged a history student exchange.

"We also have students from America and most of Europe, which is a revolutionary change for the college, even in the context of the past ten years," he said.

Change is a constant element of the academic discipline embraced by Liam Irwin and his particular expertise is concerned very much with the relevence of the past to the present and to the future.

In a broader context history can not only direct us, but provide lessons for the future. It is a point he puts well: "In history we argue that the past is very relevant, but it is very much the relevance of the past to the present and to the future. This idea is far more recognised now."

The close working relationship between the history departments of the college and the University is illustrated in plans for a new joint masters degree in local history. He feels that a major change in Limerick is the greater interest in heritage, in every respect; buildings, history and the whole self-confidence of the city.

"I must be one of the few who does not hate that interpretative centre in King John's Castle," he smiles. "I'm not saying that I love it either, but I'm not offended by it. When you go inside you can see the archaeology underneath in situ and that is important."

It is not so long ago that Liam Irwin as Secretary of the Thomond Archaeological Society was described as a trouble maker when the organisation queried the actions of public officials. Today conflict has been replaced by consultation.

Liam Irwin feels that it is easy to have a concern for archaeology if the economy is doing well, but warns of the consequences of an economic downturn: "If money is scarce there is a danger that the spectre of the 1930s may return when - in the ethos of the time - they built all the corporation houses in the middle of King John's Castle. Perhaps something as extreme as that would not happen again, but I think continued vigilance is necessary."

When he is not "down a hole in the ground" Liam Irwin likes to walk for relaxation, attends the theatre, visits art galleries, reads and keeps up with current affairs.

"In Ireland today - and what we are going through at the moment - you don't need to preach the message that the past affects the way we are, or where we are going..."

In conversation with Frank Hamilton

Raoul Peter Jackson

My father, the artist, Raoul Peter Jackson (known to some as 'the Raoul'), was born in Limerick city on 13 October, 1946. His father was an English merchant seaman, Raoul Jackson. His mother was Myra Ryan of Rosbrien. Peter who was the youngest of three children, grew up on Carey's Road. He also spent much of his time with his Spanish grandmother, Dolores Rodriguez Jackson, well-known as a flamenco dancer of earlier days.

Peter went to Leamy's School and in 1964 entered the Limerick School Of Art, where he studied under Jack Donovan. The famous Yorkshire water-colourist, Ashley Jackson, was Peter's first cousin. Art was in his blood, but at this time, he was also preoccupied with his music.

He was quite involved in the Limerick music scene of the time. He was resident DJ at Club-A-Go-Go in the Sixties and was involved in many bands of his own such as, Peter's Tweeds and Peter and The Wolves. He toured as a drummer with Craig Douglas and played with the College Showband and the Jack Glynn Quintet. His love of percussion began with the Boherbuoy Band. His greatest drumming moment was during the 1967 Festival of Shannonside, when he attempted to break the solo drumming world record of thirty-six hours non-stop in Jack Glynn's shop window.

Peter never forgot great moments and memories - people's names weren't always as fortunate. I remember once being introduced to a prospective painting-buyer called Oscar. It wasn't until later on,

"Oh Dad! Don't bring the paintings. We're going on holidays," I remember saying one summer as we headed on a family holiday. I knew even then, as an eight-year-old girl, how much art meant to my father.

that I discovered that "Oscar's" name was actually Vincent. Dad had gotten his name wrong while introducing him.

Peter's enthusiasm for art was obvious in his work. According to the Limerick poet and his close friend, Dr. Desmond O'Grady, his work always reflected "a youthful freshness and wonder". In the early seventies, Peter lived with Desmond O'Grady in Rome and on the Greek island of Paros. On returning from Greece, he met Aideen O'Sullivan, in Limerick whilst on a double date. They married in 1977.

In 1982, they moved to Hospital, where Peter devoted himself to painting full-time. The family moved to Lough Gur in 1989, now with daughter and son, Cathy and Barry, in tow. In 1993 they opened their own studio and gallery in Lough Gur.

Peter especially loved the beauty and mysticism of Lough Gur, the Burren and Carnac, which inspired many of his paintings. Despite his love for Lough Gur, he was a Limerick City boy at heart.

This was to end, however, when Peter died suddenly on 9 June, 1996. The man, described by one of his friends as "an advertisement for life", had been robbed of his life, so young, so suddenly and so tragically. However, in his forty-nine years, he had lived life to the full in a way that most could only hope to do in twice that amount of time. He had answered his vocation to be an artist. The family that was his love, art that was his obsession and Limerick and his friends that were his life, will always remember him for this.

Remembered by Cathy Jackson

Dermot Kelly

Dermot Kelly, affectionately referred to as "The Singing Bank Manager", is probably best known in Limerick for his long career as a banker and entertainer. His working life was spent with the Bank of Ireland; forty-two years in total, mainly in and around the city. "These were good times", he recalls, "and it was through the bank that I met many of my best friends".

On completing his daily duties in the financial world, Dermot could tune into his greatest hobby; singing and songwriting. His compositions include *Limerick, My Home*, the story of an emigrant who is returning home to Limerick, and *Joe McHugh*, a song about the famous Liscannor publican. Others include *Cliffs of Moher, Rise Up John Reilly* and *Smiling Christy Junior*, a tribute to the great golfer, Christy O'Connor Junior. With the help of Denis Allen, he has recorded two tapes, featuring a large selection of his works. He has also appeared on RTE's *Late Late Show*, Donncha O'Dulaing, Bibi and Liam O Murchú, and was formerly a member of Limerick's College Players.

"My most amusing recording is about the mighty Cork hurler, Christy Ring. It is called *The Day that Christy Ring gave up the Hurling to do the Rock 'n' Roll*", he says enthusiastically before breaking into song. Although now retired, the fresh sixty-three year old loves life now as much as ever.

LIMERICK, MY HOME

*Limerick, you're my
  City, I'm coming
  home to you,
Across the broad
  Atlantic, I'll bid New
  York adieu,
My heart is beating
  faster, I think about
  you all,
Celebrating Sarsfield
  and the women on
  the wall.*

*Is the Treaty Stone
  still standing? Is
  the castle looking
  fine?
Do the boys still drink
  at Angela's? How
  are they in the Isle?
Will ye meet me at the
  airport? I'll be shy
  and ill-at-ease,
Limerick, I love you,
  your gentle
  Shannon breeze.*

*How is the River
  Shannon, stealing
  to the sea,
Carrying the memories
  of our proud
  history,
Kings and merchant
  princes, sportsmen
  warriors true,
Limerick, I love you,
  I'm coming home to
  you.*

In the sporting arena, Dermot has also made his mark. Dermot Kelly will always be remembered as the Limerick hurler who scored one goal and twelve points against Clare in the Munster Hurling Championship of 1955. To this day, he still holds the record for the highest number of scores in a Munster Final. Four Railway Cup Medals in the 1950s and a term as Limerick County Captain in 1956, together with hurlers such as Ring, Doyle and Stakelum are other memories that he cherishes. "I also have great memories of playing football with the Claughaun Club as a boy, and have remained in contact with the club down through the years". Dermot also holds a Bravery Award for a sea rescue in Ballybunion in 1951.

Nowadays, Dermot has moved on to other sporting interests, with golf in the number one position. The Kellys' second home in Lahinch serves as a perfect excuse for Dermot, formerly Captain of both Lahinch and Ennis Clubs, to keep up his golf, while also enjoying the scenery and people of the West of Ireland, which are close to his heart.

With their family of six now reared, Dermot, together with his wife, Breda, travel far and wide. "However, we always end up back in Limerick and love it too much to stay away for very long."

Dermot's own composition, *Limerick, My Home* says it all for him.

In conversation with Mal Keaveney

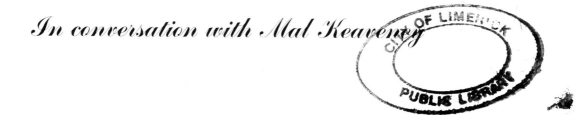

Jim Kemmy

It would not be an exaggeration to say that Jim Kemmy has dedicated virtually his whole life to politics, Limerick, and particularly to the people of Limerick. Nobody could love this city more or talk about it with such reverence than he. His own personal ambitions are few; but his aspirations for Limerick and its people are many.

Reared in Limerick, Jim feels it is now a finer place to live than it was, say, fifty years ago.

He has just completed his second term of office as mayor and while he didn't expect to become mayor so quickly after his last term, he typically was manifestly honoured to fulfil the office during the 1995 and 1996 period.

Jim has seen many changes over the years. The last six years have been the most significant. He referred to the modern City Hall, the new Regional Technical College, the first phase of the Northern Relief Road, the £15 million library at the University, the major extension at the Regional Hospital and myriad other projects that are presently at an advanced stage.

> **"If you look at the skyline of Limerick, six large cranes over building projects tell their own story of a city on the move."**

Limerick's amazing sporting record over the last number of years has given him cause for great joy: "Limerick's rugby teams have been supreme and our hurlers are well on their way to a long awaited All-Ireland title."

He speaks with extreme pride about the cultural life of the city, which he says has never been better. "The University Concert Hall has been a terrific asset and amenity to the community. Our amateur theatrical groups have also been very successful. The College Players have won awards both nationally and internationally. All other groups in the city are very active."

Jim declared: "Next year represents a fine opportunity for Limerick to put its best foot forward when the city celebrates its 800th anniversary as a chartered city. I believe it will be an exciting and eventful year for Limerick. Already a committee is in place to co-ordinate the various activities, but it is important that all groups and individuals make a special effort to celebrate the year." Jim naturally will be playing an active part himself in the celebrations.

Well-known for his literary skills, Jim has an anthology on the point of publication. Approached by Gill & Macmillan to compile an anthology of Limerick writings over the centuries, he now has enough material left over for a second book, provided his first one is sufficiently successful. He has also plans to publish a special edition of the *Old Limerick Journal* covering the granting of the charter to Limerick in 1197 and Limerick's civic life down through the centuries.

He has many other plans for the year and does not intend being a passive observer of this unique and most significant year in Limerick's long history.

A controversial figure in the media, Jim hit the headlines when he spoke out about Ireland's "moving statues". A stonemason himself, he was well aware that statues have no powers of locomotion. He kept a low profile during the frenzy, but when asked by a journalist about the phenomenon he described it as "nonsense" and "self-delusional". For his pains he was roundly criticised, but says that the statues have not gone on a walkabout since!

Jim will have to contend with a general election next year and will be battling energetically to retain his Dáil seat. "Limerick is always a volatile constituency and I expect it will live up to its reputation in this regard next time out."

In conversation with Eileen Brophy

Mike Keyes

"We thought it would be an effective way of addressing the male/female imbalance in our club in the early days, and the name has since stuck!" This is how Limerickman, Mike Keyes, explains the origins of the rather unusual name of the club that he co-founded in 1981; The Limerick Climbing and Crochet Club. Judging from its weekly, Thursday-night gatherings in Flannery's pub on Catherine Street, the ploy seems to have worked very well indeed. "If anything, we now have more female than male members, but we're not complaining! We all share a common interest and goal; that is, to climb mountains and enjoy ourselves", he explains.

An in-built desire to constantly seek out new challenges, combined with a love of being in beautiful places has landed Mike Keyes on the top of almost all of Ireland's principal peaks. He has also gone on several climbing trips to the UK and continental Europe, and in 1992, fulfilled a lifelong ambition by planning and completing a climb, together with four others, in the Himalayas. "The six-week trip took eighteen months to plan. In addition to the extensive paperwork, route planning and demanding training programme, seeking out corporate sponsorship to help cover the expedition costs also took a lot of time. We even camped out overnight once in a refrigerated warehouse to test out our gear before leaving, which raised one or two eyebrows at the time!", Mike recalls.

Despite the fact that adverse weather conditions prevented the mountaineers from completing the last stage of the climb to 7,200 metre-high Masherbum II peak, Mike's overriding memories of the trip are tremendous.

As chairman of the Mountaineering Council of Ireland (MCI) since January 1994, Mike has seen its membership grow to an all time high of 4,200, representing an increase of over twenty-five percent in less than two years. He points out, that contrary to the common perception of mountaineering as an extremely risky and somewhat foolhardy pastime, the number of accidents overall are very low. "Mountaineering includes everything from leisurely hillside rambles to scaling up vertical rock faces. Our members are encouraged to gain the necessary mountain skills, and then use common sense in matching up the chosen mountaineering activities with their own capabilities.

"The challenge doesn't really lie in the peaks themselves, but in the way each individual sets out to climb them."

One of the highlights of Mike's term as chairman of MCI has been to see the relocation of the council's collection of books to the library at the University of Limerick.

An architectural technician by profession, Indian cooking, music and travel are amongst the other activities which mountaineer Mike enjoys in his spare time. A competent flautist, he has fond memories of his days touring around Germany as a member of traditional group, *Cromlach*, in the '70s. Famed for their dancer, Más Dálaigh, Mike stakes his claim, that his people were the forerunners of *Riverdance!*

Nowadays, however, he is happy to be in Limerick, but looks forward to the prospect of returning some day to Asia, together with his wife, Marian, and children, Seán and Eva.

In conversation with Mary Fennelly

Gary Kirby

Down the years, hurling has been embroidered by players of outstanding quality - wonderful leadership - love of the game - parish as well as county pride - exemplary sportsmanship and a willingness to meet the challenge of the game at club level and the more demanding challenge at inter-county level. Such a player is Gary Kirby.

Since bursting upon the scene in 1981, when he helped his native Patrickswell to city under-16 honours, Gary has commanded a special place in the hearts of Limerick's hurling fraternity. One of the outstanding modern day hurlers, acknowledged as such, beyond the confines of his own county, his contribution to Limerick knows no bounds. He is totally dedicated to hurling and uses every possible occasion to promote and seek support for hurling at under-age level.

"If hurling is to survive in a time of change as we are experiencing coming up to the third millenium, it is vitally important that our young players are taught the skills of the game, as well as a love of the ancient craft. We should make use of every exposure available in the ongoing work to win the hearts and minds of our young people."

"There is a huge battle being fought for the backing of the boys and girls, who will be the players of tomorrow, be it hurling, soccer, rugby, or indeed many other pastimes. If we lose our young people to other games, it will be at the expense of our own national pastime."

This is the clear message from Gary, who is confident that Limerick is providing this leadership and doing the work to keep hurling at the top of the sporting agenda. And he finds time to do his own bit for Patrickswell, despite his many commitments to club and county. Camogie in the "Well" is currently going through a good spell and Gary is there to lend a hand at coaching or advising the girls.

Already the holder of three All Star awards, he has made the centre forward position his own on the Limerick team, since winning an All Ireland Minor in 1984 and an under-21 in 1987. One man does not make a team, although at times this theory verges on collapse, when Gary turns on the style.

Hurling has been good to Gary. His treasure trove includes All Stars, three Railway Cups, National Leagues, Minor and Under-21 All Irelands, County medals with Patrickswell in Minor, under-21 and senior and he captained Ireland in under-21 shinty in 1987 against Scotland. He counts this game in the Highlands as one of his most memorable moments. He played senior shinty in Galway in 1984 and was an All Star replacement in 1989.

Gary, who married Carmel Cronin of Kinsale in the early months of 1996, is a son of Patrick and Angela. His father is a keen hurling enthusiast and his mother is a sister of Phil Bennis.

Gary captained in 1994, demonstrating his wonderful qualities as a leader. That dramatic comeback by Offaly - snatching what seemed certain victory in the closing minutes, would have shattered the bravest of players, but Gary took it like the sportsman he is and vowed he would again grace Croke Park in the Limerick colours.

Gary has won a special niche in the annals of hurling. His dynamic leadership, his ability on the field of play and his pursuit of the highest accolade of the game, places him on the same pedestal as the Howards, Mackeys, Grimes and Cregans of other eras.

In conversation with Harry Greensmyth

Dr. Peter Kirwan

Psychiatrist Dr. Peter Kirwan is fiercely passionate about his work, and particularly so about bringing mental health care out of the dark ages. But his one main aim and hope is soon to be realised and that is the ultimate closure of the city's most stark and dreary reminder of what psychiatric care used to be like. The very physical appearance of St. Joseph's Hospital suggests that it is a place frozen in the 1800s. Its high grey walls and railings, barred windows, and yawning, cut-stone Dickensian facade all combine to give the appearance of a jail. Inside, there is a capacity to hold 1,000 patients, and in 1981, when Dr. Kirwan, who is originally from Dublin, first began practising at the Limerick Regional Hospital's psychiatric unit, there were still 800 patients living there.

Now there are just over 200, and the numbers are steadily decreasing as it is now the Health Department's policy to finally close all such institutions. The 600 have now all been either placed in smaller hostel-type institutions, catering for approximately fifteen in-patients where they have their own private living quarters, moved to half-way houses where six or so patients live together in relative independence or have been sent to live with their families or alone, just attending clinics as out-patients. This is Dr. Kirwan's dream coming true. He passionately believes that proper care of the mentally ill, to whatever degree, depends on them being integrated into society, and not shut away, literally behind bars.

Society in general he believes, is still nervous and somewhat afraid of mental illness, although there are certain areas which are no longer taboo. Depression for example is something which used to be a darkly kept secret, but now people can openly talk about it and seek treatment without feeling in any way ashamed. "AWARE, the support organisation for people who suffer from depression is to be thanked a lot for this step forward," he says.

"St. Joseph's was designed to house people in conditions that are far from humane, to shut them away from society. I want to destigmatise mental illness and in order to do this, sufferers must be rehoused in conditions that give them the dignity they are entitled to."

Dr. Kirwan, who is married to a former nurse and has two children, fully supports the design of the psychiatric unit at the Regional Hospital, and it is this development which Dr. Kirwan looks forward to seeing more of nationally. In every way more like a hotel than a psychiatric hospital. A far cry indeed from the high-ceilinged echoing corridors and flaking government green paint of St. Joseph's.

But there is a lot more to Dr. Kirwan than the dedicated psychiatrist. He's a bubbly, confident man who enjoys gentle hill-walking in what he describes as his cultural home, Kerry, and is positively addicted to the Irish language.

After his father's death from heart disease, his mother, a working GP, like her late husband, reluctantly had to send all but one of her four children to boarding school. While Peter's two brothers seemed to be content in Mungret College, the four years that he spent there were concentrated at best on longing for the summers in Kerry and at worst on planning his escape. Twice he managed to run away, and it is perhaps how he felt like a prisoner that he now actively loathes the old method of housing and caring for psychiatric patients.

In conversation with Claire Connolly Doyle

Pat Lawless

"I was never lonely", said veteran sailor Pat Lawless of his record-breaking solo voyage around the world. Arriving into Kilrush Creek Marina last summer to a hero's welcome, after sailing singlehandedly around the globe in a modest thirty-foot boat, seventy-year-old Pat again set foot on Irish soil after an absence of three years and two days.

Looking remarkably fresh and healthy (his son Dan described him as "like a two-year-old"), Pat greeted his friends and well-wishers warmly, before being whisked away for a series of media interviews. Hailed as Ireland's "other gold medallist" (Michelle Smith had just won three gold medals at the Olympics), Pat was his usual humorous and unassuming self. Typically, he made light of his enormous achievement, joining the elite group of top-class sailors who have successfully circumnavigated the globe single-handedly.

"I'm getting a bit long in the tooth. Let's just say I've no immediate plans to go off again."

Speaking later of what it was like to be alone at sea for months on end, Pat said he would send a message to his family via a passing ship whenever possible, assuring them he was alright. But this one-way communication often proved frustrating - he would worry about his family thousands of miles away - his wife Nancy, sister Betty, five sons and one daughter, and nine grandchildren, some of whom had grown so much he would hardly recognise them. And yet he was never lonely. Inexplicably to a non-sailor, he was kept very busy all day long in sailing the boat and keeping her on course and in order.

During what was the first reunion of the entire Lawless clan in a decade, including son Jim, who planned his return to Ireland after ten years in Bahrain to coincide with his father's homecoming, Pat savoured his first pint of Guinness on Irish soil in three years. He is very grateful to his loyal supporters and sponsors in Limerick, including his friend and next-door neighbour, Tony O'Mara of Toyota Limerick, and John Hunt of Craggaunowen, appropriately the home of the Brendan Boat. He received many telegrams and messages of congratulations, including one from fellow yachtsman, Charles J. Haughey and from President Mary Robinson.

"I've seen the oceans - I'm happy", said Pat. "I can't believe I'm with my loved ones again".

Born in Liverpool of a Dublin father and a Limerick mother, Pat spent his early years in Dalkey, County Dublin, but the family then moved to his beloved Limerick, where his grandfather was secretary of the Harbour Board.

Pat's enthusiasm for the sea surfaced very early, but his mother arranged for the sixteen-year-old's application for a job as an able-bodied seaman to be rejected, and he became a cabinet-maker instead. But it was a futile effort and Pat's love of all things nautical culminated in three attempts to sail around the world, including the third successful one, and no fewer than five crossings of the Atlantic.

Pat's historic voyage took him to Madeira, South Africa, Australia, Tasmania, New Zealand, Chile, Equador and Panama, where he celebrated his seventieth birthday on St. Patrick's Day, then on to the Cayman Islands and Florida, his last stop, before setting sail home to Ireland.

Pat's wife Nancy is philosophical about his yearning for the sea. "I never tried to stop him", she says, "because I knew it was impossible".

Unbelievably, Pat will not rule out a further voyage.

In conversation with Marian Malone

Venerable Archdeacon Michael Manning

The slight hint of a Cork accent still indicates that Michael Manning has roots in the county and his fondness for mentioning Glanmire betrays the fact that he was born there, at Brook Lodge, some seventy years ago. However as soon as you engage him in recalling his background, he will turn his mind to West Limerick, to Clouneagh, to Tiernahilla, where his mother, Mary came from and to Dromcollogher, where he spent much of his youth. A strong sense of roots in his family meant that he went to secondary school in St. Munchin's College, and, eventually, when he decided to study for the priesthood, he went to Maynooth as a student of the Diocese of Limerick. When he was ordained in 1951, he went to U.C.C. to study for the Higher Diploma in Education and while there he taught in St. Finbar's, Farranferris. On his return to the Diocese of Limerick, he was appointed to the staff of St. Munchin's College. However his heart was in pastoral work rather than in teaching and in 1952 he was appointed to St. Michael's Parish, Limerick.

It was a vibrant parish, with many sporting and social facilities for the youth. Fr. Manning, as the junior curate, was given particular care of the Boy Scouts and St. Michael's Temperance Society. His enthusiasm for his work and his genuine commitment to the welfare of the young made for him friendships which have lasted a lifetime.

For twenty one years, Fr. Manning served the large parish of St. Michael's, living in Barrington Street, in that large house which stands at the end of the Tontine in Pery Square. He was host to innumerable people; rich and poor came to tell him their troubles; clergy and lay people, young and old, came to share a meal with the 'men of St. Michael's", as the priests there were called.

In 1973 he became the first resident parish priest of St. Michael's in almost one-hundred-and-fifty years. Bishop Murphy, shortly before he died, decided that with urban development, the original parish was too large. Fr. Liam Boyle became the new administrator of St. Joseph's and Fr. Manning left Barrington Street and went to live in Sexton Street, in a house quite near the old St. Michael's Presbytery, which had by then become the Presentation Convent. There he continued his pastoral work until 1979, when he was appointed parish priest of St. Munchin's.

He is a people's priest, known and loved at home and abroad. A great Churchman, he wears his distinction lightly.

Above all the archdeacon is a devout and a peoples' priest. His personal faith in Lourdes and in St. Anne de Beaupre, reflect his Marian devotion. For many years, late on a Sunday night, he could be heard listening to tapes of talks given by Bishop Fulton Sheen. Evening Prayer, the official prayer of the Church, was said on a regular basis by his fellow priests in St. Michael's. His homilies, which sometimes stretched a little, were, nevertheless full of sympathy and human wisdom. Occasionally people did not like what they heard, rarely was it far from the truth.

His care for the sick and the dying, his willingness to travel long distances to comfort the bereaved, his special way with young people and young priests, his interest in what was the Catholic Marriage Advisory Council and the Adoption Board, together with his wide range of contacts, has won for him an international reputation.

Reflections with three colleagues

Jerry McCabe

Death came to a popular and much-loved garda in one of Ireland's most beautiful villages during a deadly attack.

Detective Garda Jerry McCabe and his colleague, Detective Garda Ben O'Sullivan, were escorting an early morning post office delivery truck in Adare when Jerry was fatally wounded and Ben received serious injuries. The unsuspecting gardaí stood no chance when powerful Kalashnikovs opened up on them.

Jerry McCabe was fifty-two, a garda going about his duties with his colleague. He was dedicated to his work and was a proud man the day his son joined the Force.

Jerry was a friend to everybody and the warmth of his personality endeared him to colleagues and to top-level politicians who had the pleasure of having him as an escort. Among the tributes paid to him was one by former Northern Secretary, Tom King MP. He had been accompanied by Jerry during the British-Irish interparliamentary meeting earlier that year, in the self-same village where Jerry was killed.

A Kerryman born in Ballybunion, the family moved to Ballylongford where his father Johnny ran a newsagency and grocery business. His schooling brought him to Rockwell College and UCC and as a twenty-year-old, he joined the Garda Síochána.

Having served in various locations, he married Ann in 1967 and joined the Detective Branch in June 1973. Jerry was known to friends and neighbours alike as a happy man 'full of devilment' and wit and mad for *craic*. He was a man of ingenuity and if there was a problem, Jerry was called in. He came to the rescue of family and neighbours with his "great hands" and could fix anything from a washing machine to a motor car.

The shock and revulsion felt by the shootings was demonstrated in the huge turnout for the dead garda's funeral, including dignitaries and the plain people of Ireland paying their last respects.

Jerry was proud father to John (27), a garda, Mark (25), an electrician, Ian (24), a University of Limerick graduate in Public Administration, Stacy (17), a student at the Salesian Secondary School, Fernbank and Ross (16) who attends Árd Scoil Rís. He was known as a devoted father and family man for thirty years and his son John described him as follows:

> "Each one of us always felt very special to him and as we grew, our relationships with him developed into ones of friendship as well as family."
> Garda John McCabe speaking of his late father, Jerry.

"I know that I speak for my sister and brothers when I say that we have a tremendous pride in everything Dad did from career to golf. As adults, we now see that who we have become results from many years of love, patience and hard work by both Mom and Dad".

A college fellowship today honours the memory of the slain garda. The McCabe Fellowship was established by the John Jay College of Criminal Justice, part of the City University of New York and the Garda Síochána. It provides for the regular exchange of students and the first recipient of the fellowship was Garda John McCabe.

Well-known Auctioneer, Pat Kearney, paying tribute to his late brother-in-law at the funeral Mass encapsulated Jerry the man thus: "Jerry was our friend, we miss him greatly, God rest him".

Remembered by James O'Brien

Audrey McCormack

Limerick lace-making was all but dead when Audrey McCormack from Janesboro took part in a twelve-month course in the craft in 1987. Today she is one of very few people in Limerick making the traditional lace, having revived a craft long synonymous with the Treaty City.

Although many Limerick people would have heard about Limerick lace, most would never have seen it and would know very little of its background. Audrey explained that Limerick had one of the first commercial lace-making ventures in Ireland, following the establishment of a factory here in 1829 by Charles Walker, a native of Oxford. Most of the produce was exported to England, where there was a ready-made market. Over the years, the industry in Limerick experienced a gradual decline as cheaper, machine-made produce entered the market from the middle of the nineteenth century. However, the efforts of Florence Vere O'Brien in the 1888s, and the nuns at the Good Shepherd Convent in the 1850s, ensured that the tradition was not lost forever. "To this day, Limerick lace is on display in the Good Shepherd Convent", Audrey confirmed.

"Limerick Lace is quite easy to make, but the process is slow and tedious, and requires a lot of patience!"

Influenced by her mother, Angela, Audrey recalled her interest in the craft beginning at an early age, when she first saw samples of Limerick lace. The way it is made is unusual and the end product is very fine, delicate and unique. It is still made with the same materials and techniques used in the past, cotton net, cotton thread, large darning needles, lace scissors and wooden rectangular frame, similar to an embroidery frame.

Prompted by the fact that it was almost impossible to buy a piece of Limerick lace in the city during the late 1980s, on completing her lace-making course, Audrey and fellow student, Mary Power, set up a business to make the lace commercially. However, despite having received assistance and great encouragement from Shannon Development, they were unable to make a reasonable living from it, and discontinued with the venture after three years.

Nevertheless, Audrey was determined to continue with the craft to keep it alive. With the constant pressure of deadlines and making a living gone, she could take her time and enjoy it. Then fate gave a hand, when she received a box of old patterns for the traditional Limerick lace from a lady in the county. "I then came up with the idea of producing popular lace products part-time, which would make Limerick lace more affordable and more widely available", Audrey recalled. In 1993, she started selling samples of lace displayed in small, oval frames. The concept worked well, and to this day, they can be seen at tourist outlets and shops throughout the region, thereby keeping the old craft in the eye of both natives and visitors to the city. Audrey also makes special pieces on commission, whenever time permits.

"I would love to go back into making Limerick lace full-time again", she said, looking to the future. "I would also like to run some classes in the craft. In order to really revive Limerick lace-making, more people must learn to make it. Otherwise, it will die and will be lost forever".

In conversation with Billy Kelly

Maeve Mc Cormack Nolan

"I am a people and flowers person" is how artist Maeve McCormack Nolan describes herself, her garden, ablaze with the colour combinations of late summer blossoms. Once inside the house, a truly magnificent collection of paintings takes up every square inch of space along the hallway - all Maeve's own work. An even greater number and variety of her paintings awaits in the sitting room, mainly of colourful bouquets of flowers done in oils, with a few landscapes interspersed, one more beautiful than the next.

The sheer volume of paintings is indicative of the infinite hours that Maeve spends at her easel. "After my guys, (referring to husband and son, both called Val), painting is the most important thing in my life. It takes me onto a different plain". Whereas most artists strive for peaceful surroundings, Maeve is at her most creative when she can keep in touch with the comings and goings of her loved ones, and therefore usually paints in the family dining room.

Looking at her face, alight with enthusiasm and the obvious delight at bringing someone new into her colourful world, one almost overlooks the fact that Maeve has suffered from multiple sclerosis for more than twenty years - half of her lifetime. Although she now depends on a walking aid to get from A to B and has lost eighty percent of her vision as a result of the illness, she is determined to get on with life and refuses to crumble beneath it.

"My late father, Paddy, gave me my great love of life and of nature. If I cannot get over something, I'll always find some way of getting around it."

This love of life exudes from the prolific artist as she talks about her life, her family and her work. The subject of considerable media coverage, she has exhibited her works extensively in Ireland and overseas, including three prestigious Guinness Hopstore exhibitions. Maeve has also developed the mono-dual-acrylic technique, which is unique to her and forms the basis for her corporate works.

"I think of myself as an artist first, and then as being disabled. I don't like the label people sometimes put on those of us with a disability". Maeve continues to be amused by people's attitudes towards the disabled, and recounts an incident when she once visited a Limerick café with a friend. "Does she take tea or coffee?," the waitress uttered distinctly, while looking Maeve's companion in the eye. "Tea please," replied Maeve assuredly, puzzled as to why she hadn't been asked directly in the first place.

Guided by the principle that her last painting must always be her best, Maeve plans to extend the range of greeting cards, that she started to supply to leading stationery outlets countrywide in 1995, to include even more of her floral works. Over and above this, however, her main ambition is to be able to continue her happy lifestyle and hang onto her independence for as long as is humanly possible. *"Go mbeirimíd beo ar an am seo arís ...* and vertical", she chuckles.

In conversation with Mary Fennelly

Kay McGuinness

Kay McGuinness is undoubtedly one of the most prominent figures in the Limerick Business World. Not only is she president of the chamber of commerce, but she has also been managing director of one of the most successful advertising agencies outside of Dublin, Southern Advertising.

Kay was born in the Alexandra Nursing Home in O'Connell Avenue. Her father was in the army and the family lived in Ballinacurra and then in Sarsfield Barracks.

After secondary school in Laurel Hill, Kay went on to do a secretarial course in The High School or Mac's as it was affectionately known. "Mrs. Mac is really proud of me" Kay says laughing. "I suppose she sees me as one of her many successes. I joined CIE in Colbert Station. It was good fun and I gained lots of experience. There were always interesting people passing through." Eventually the advertising agency O'Kennedy Brindly opened in Limerick and they were looking for a 'girl Friday'. The rest we suppose is history."

"There's a famous saying in the advertising business that goes 'Advertising is the most fun you can have with your clothes on' and I have to agree."

In 1979 O'Kennedy Brindly was taken over by the advertising gurus Saatchi & Saatchi, leaving O'Kennedy Brindly Cork up for grabs. Kay and three of her colleagues took the opportunity and bought the company. "It simply was a case of being in the right place at the right time" says Kay. "Of course we had to change the name. It's the trend amongst advertising agencies to name themselves after the partners, but ours didn't gel right, so we eventually decided on Southern Advertising, which is fine except when you get clients in the North. Usually when we go north these days we go under the name of S.A. Group, it's a bit more tactful".

"The basic principles of advertising haven't changed over the years. The main change I've seen was the introduction of local radio, which has become a very welcome addition to the media mix. I spent five years on the RTE Authority which was brilliant experience.

I don't think the print media should be nervous of the electronic media. Each is an entirely different medium, and there will always be a strong case for print advertising.

It is also one of the service industries in which women really have excelled. I feel this is because we pay far greater attention to detail and are driven by our emotions. Advertising is all about appealing to emotions."

As well as being an advertising woman, Kay also influences business developments in the Mid-West Region due to her work with the Limerick Chamber of Commerce. The introduction of a second air carrier on the Shannon London Route was one of the issues she lobbied strongly for. She is passionate about the need for urban renewal in the heart of Limerick City and the reinstatement of some civic pride. "We have so much going for us here, especially in the music and sports scenes, I think we should enjoy ourselves without being so defensive to outsiders. All cities share the common problems of drugs and violence. We need to be pro-active not reactive".

Having lived all her life in Limerick, Kay has never thought of any reason to leave. "I have done pretty well here", she says, "and it is my home. My mother is living on the Ennis Road. My work is here. Limerick is a fine spot, why would I want to live anywhere else?"

In conversation with Valerie O'Connor

Barbara McMahon

Ireland's best dressed lady came from Dundalk to the Shannon Region in 1969. Barbara McMahon was drawn to this part of the world to work with the castle entertainers in Bunratty, Knappogue and Dunguire Castles. "It was love at first sight" smiles Barbara, as she remembers the early days of Limerick life, "Marcus saw a picture of me in medieval costume and fell in love!". Four months later, Barbara was destined for a future in Limerick. Now living in her Castleconnell home with Marcus, her husband and their three children, Barbara describes her life as "very busy but very happy".

Settling into a new city was not difficult for Barbara. She credits much of her expediency in adapting to the change, to the friendliness of the Limerick people, with whom she has made many close friends. 'Energised' best sums up this active woman, who manages to balance family life with a hectic work schedule and still look glamorous and vivacious. Probably best known for her work with the RTE production *Head to Toe*, Barbara has been part of the presenting and researching team for eight years. Travelling to Dublin by train on Sunday returning on Wednesday evening is the routine for Barbara seven months a year. "RTE have been very good to me. They have always accommodated my needs and are a wonderful organisation to work with." Her praise for the national station is impressive. "I get my brief and am let to run with it."

RTE 'discovered' her natural talent for presenting when she appeared on *Live at Three's* enterprise spot. For some years previously, Barbara had studied interior design. While promoting her new product, a bedside table, on the afternoon show, the producers were so impressed with her ability to present that they recommended she apply for a presenter's position with the organisation. Her application was one of four thousand. It was three years later when RTE contacted her to participate with fifteen other applicants, in a presenter's course. Upon completion, she alone was chosen as a presenter and in 1989 *Head to Toe* was launched with Barbara McMahon at the helm.

Although she describes herself as "not an expert on fashion or style", Barbara admits to loving it. "I really appreciate good quality and design, whether it be in clothes or house decor," she said, referring back to her professional background. Her work has appeared in the USA's well known *House Beautiful* magazine.

> "Limerick should be proud of its contribution to the world of fashion. This is now internationally recognised."

Fitness and health are an important part of the McMahon lifestyle. Walking every day with *Quilty* the family dog keeps this active woman in shape, along with gardening and playing tennis during her free summer months. Her ideal social event consists of meeting with family and close friends; "A log fire, with a gale force wind blowing outside and a good movie on television."

Barbara praises her adopted home. "Both city and county have had many achievements and awards associated with them over the past number of years. The profile of Limerick has been lifted with all the structural changes taking place within the city. Also, the friendliness of the people cannot be overlooked". While she claims to have no crystal ball, Barbara is willing to go where the wind takes her with her career.

In conversation with Linda Lane

Suzanne Murphy

Limerick's Suzanne Murphy is universally acclaimed as one of the finest sopranos in the world.

She has sung at Buckingham Palace, at a private dinner for the Queen of Denmark, entertained the King and Queen of Sweden, and been invited to sing for important guests of the British Prime Minister at 10 Downing Street.

Among her appreciative audiences have been the Prince and Princess of Wales, Prince and Princess Michael of Kent, Baroness Margaret Thatcher and President Mary Robinson.

She's in constant demand to sing leading roles in a variety of languages, in all of the world's famous Opera Houses and modestly admits that her engagement book is full for the next two years.

In spite of all this success, Suzanne remains the same friendly, modest person she was, when she started her singing career with the Cecilian Musical Society in Limerick, over thirty years ago.

"As a child, one of my greatest treats during the Easter holidays, was to be taken to see the current production of the Cecilians at the Crescent Theatre", she recalls. "The minute I left Bruff boarding school, I auditioned to join the society and was thrilled to be accepted for the ladies' chorus. In my first year with them, I was given a comic role in the operetta, *Naughty Marietta* and that was it. I was stage struck!"

Suzanne decided to take singing lessons with Mrs Baker, who taught in O'Connell Street, near where

> "Limerick means so much to me, that I gave the name, *There Is an Isle* to my album of classical Irish songs. I just love Limerick and its people."

Suzanne had a job with an insurance company. Suzanne asked her if she had the talent to become professional. "I'll always remember her reply. 'You don't have the strength in your voice Suzanne, it's too pink and white'! I often smile now at the memory".

Soon, the bright lights of Dublin beckoned and Suzanne took a job with an insurance firm in the city. "I still loved singing and was part of the very successful 'We 4' folk group, with Larry Hogan, John Harrington, Denis Howatt and later, Donal Lunny. However, we decided to disband the group in 1971".

Suzanne counts herself very lucky to have been accepted by Veronica Dunne for voice training at the time. Veronica persuaded Suzanne to audition for the Irish National Opera. She was successful and gave up her insurance job to sing full time.

In 1976, Suzanne auditioned for the Welsh National Opera and was offered a contract as one of their principal sopranos. "I stayed with them, singing leading roles in all their operas, until my contract finished in 1983. Then, I made the big decision to go freelance".

Since then, the offers have flooded in. Suzanne gets home to Limerick as often as she can.

"Each time I come home, I drive around the North Circular Road and note the amazing changes, and remember how, as children, we roller-skated down that road, with little or no threat of being knocked down."

In conversation with Valerie Sweeney

Pat Murray

It is little consolation for Shannon RFC full-back, Pat Murray, that he is regarded locally as Limerick's best-ever uncapped player. Consecutive seasons of top-class performances have so far failed to impress the national selectors and leading his club back to All-Ireland League victories, as well as being awarded the Irish Rugby Writers' Player of the Year in 1995, have remained unrewarded at the top level.

Pat, however, does not agree fully with those sentiments: "Better Limerick players than me have not won caps", he told us, "and while it would be nice to be honoured with selection to play for your country, I can look back on a terrific career in rugby".

Success has followed Pat throughout his career since he was first introduced to the game at St. Munchin's College in Corbally. He played soccer, hurling and football as a young primary student at Caherdavin National School and later experienced the disappointment of losing two Munster junior cup finals playing at full back with St. Munchin's College: "We went down 3-0 to Christian Brothers Cork (CBC) in the first one and lost 15-12 to Presentation Brothers Cork (PBC) the following year".

That decider remains memorable for the wrong reasons for Pat, as he had the misfortune of breaking his leg during the game, but still recovered sufficiently to sit his intermediate examination a few weeks later.

While rugby has dominated the life of the Limerick bank official, Pat has represented his county in the Munster senior football championships on two occasions, against Clare and against Tipperary. He also played soccer but since suffering a leg injury in an inter-pub game at Jackman Park some years ago, has concentrated solely on the oval ball game.

"Apart from the sporting side of rugby, there is also a terrific social side to the game, mostly in Limerick."

"Limerick is such a fantastic sports-loving city and the amount of support for rugby here is a tremendous boost for those who play the game. Hopefully the advent of professionalism will not change Limerick rugby and our teams will continue to be in the forefront of provincial and national competitions in the year to come".

Since his introduction to rugby at the age of twelve, it became clear Pat Murray was a natural footballer. Equally competent with either foot, his kicking has been a feature of his play; he is gifted with an uncanny positional sense and his tackling has never been in question. A natural leader, Pat has proven to be an outstanding club captain with the Shannon club and is acutely aware that when playing clubs outside of Limerick that the pride of his native city is very much at stake:

"I think that awareness is always there, mostly in important ties in Dublin, Belfast and Cork. Limerick is regarded nationally as the sporting capital of Ireland and our teams have a lot to live up to. I find with Shannon that we have no fear whatsoever of playing away from home."

Currently a financial adviser with the Trustee Savings Bank in Limerick, Pat said that he was "happy with the bank's general approach to their customers and their loyalty to its staff.

During his banking career, Pat took a one-year break to sample the rugby scene in New Zealand in 1988 which, he says, benefited his career significantly.

Married to Christine, Pat lives in the Corbally area, has one brother, Tom, and three sisters, Martina, Fiona and Maura.

In conversation with Aidan Corr

Gina Niland

Gina Niland came to Limerick in 1984, at the ripe old age of eleven! Having already represented Great Britain in the under twelve European Tennis championships, her dream was to make tennis her life. This dream became a reality through hours of practice and determination. Gina earned her place on the international tennis forum from her back garden tennis court in Ballyclough, County Limerick.

Born in Dublin in 1972, Gina and her family moved to Croydon in England two years later and on to Birmingham in 1976. Tennis was very much part of the Niland household, with her mother, Pat, having competed as an interprovincial player for Connaught. Her father, Ray, played Gaelic football for Mayo, and hurling for Galway.

Gina attended the Crescent Comprehensive school which provided her with an opportunity to participate in other sports. "While I very seldom trained with the team, I was a member of the senior hockey squad. My fitness through tennis practice really stood to me on the hockey pitch," recalled Gina. French was her favourite subject at school and with her mother's help, she excelled at languages. Travelling the international circuit has enabled her to use her fluent Spanish and French. "Tennis practice became as routine as homework" said Gina, "My three brothers and I played almost every day". "But it was never a chore. With Dad as my coach and advisor for the past ten years now, my success in the game is a family effort!"

Following a two year deferral period, for full-time tennis, she returned to education in 1992, taking a degree course in University College Dublin. "I chose Dublin, but not because I was anxious to leave Limerick," stated Gina. "I left not only to study Economics and French, but also to play tennis there. The indoor facilities in the capital are really good". In spite of college demands, Gina's performance in tennis went from strength to strength during her three college years. "I felt it was important to get a good education, a degree to fall back on. My parents were very strict on the education, and didn't get carried away with my dream of success!"

Gina Niland has been the number one female tennis player in Ireland since 1993 and intends to hold on to the title. Training and practice are a permanent preoccupation. When her competitive days come to an end, she looks forward to a career in coaching.

"My goal is to make a grand slam - Wimbledon, the US Open, the Australian Open and French Open within two years."

Gina has really done Limerick proud in her achievements to date. In 1986, she won the Irish Under-14 Junior Championship (Fitzwilliam) and in 1988, aged fifteen, she won the Under-18 title at Fitzwilliam. She has won the Irish Indoor Championships twice, in 1993 and 1995 and the Irish Close Championship in 1995 and 1996. Her extensive travels have allowed her to experience first hand the stress and excitement of international athletics. Taking part in the world student games in Japan in September 1995 is her most relished experience to date. This tournament is the next biggest sporting event after the Olympics. In all, 7,000 athletes participated and Ireland's number one was delighted to be counted in the last sixteen. This was not her only representation of Ireland at international level. She flew the Irish flag at the Junior Wimbledon Championship at the age of seventeen and participated at the Junior World championships in Florida 1990.

In conversation with Linda Lane

Chris Nix

In a city pulsating to a gigantic programme of commercial expansion, there is justifiable pride in being the number one man for an international company that has in its own way been part of the development.

Chris Nix, whose entire life has been involved in the social and commercial progress of his native city, while delighted with the success of the massive development plan, is anxious to ensure that the environment will retain at least some of the wonderful amenities that made his own youth a time of happy memories.

From his fourth-storey office in Mount Kennett Place, he can barely see the top of Woodcock Hill across the city skyline.

Chris' father, Bob, was a commercial traveller and an outdoor man who inspired his son with a love of flora and fauna. They lived in Shannon Terrace, on the South Circular Road and his schooling was at the Model in O'Connell Avenue and Crescent College.

Lifelong G.A.A. enthusiast, angler and wildfowler, Chris, like all conservationists, wonders about the changes on the way in the new millenium.

However, the life assurance industry beckoned him towards a career that has since been both fulfilling and successful. From a staff of four in Limerick twenty-six years ago, Canada Life has increased its workforce to twenty-five with world-wide investment now at the astonishing figure of £1.9 billion. Local investment too has soared under Chris Nix's astute direction and despite vigorous competition from banks and other financial institutions, business continues to boom for Canada Life.

Chris believes that people are now much wiser about investments and the days "when the nest egg was kept in a basket at home" are over. Last December the company moved from The Crescent to Mount Kennett.

Chris points out that since the 1970s life assurance companies have become more involved in the pension side of the business. He explains that more workers have now turned to private pensions, fearing that the state will no longer provide pensions. At the present time there are five people working for every one pensioner. Statistics show that in thirty years there will only be three workers for every one pensioner and in this situation, state pension funding couldn't be maintained. Under such circumstances retirement age would rise to seventy. "This situation has brought an urgency for private pension coverage", he says.

The rod and gun have taken care of most of his leisure hours. Mount Shannon on the shores of Lough Derg is his haunt at Mayfly time. Chris is a skilled dryfly angler and he also pursues his favourite sport of trout fishing on the Mulcair, with the occasional salmon coming to the net.

Over the winter months as a member of the Fedamore Gun Club, his greatest pleasure is watching his gun dog range across the moors and open pastures.

Chris Nix's greatest commitment to sport, however, is to the future hurlers and footballers of Mungret, where he is chairman of the G.A.A. juvenile club. "We cater for about 250 underage players - eight to sixteen year olds, both boys and girls".

Chris Nix is married to the former Edie Conway from Ballyneety. They have three girls and one boy.

In conversation with Tommy Browne

Brian O'Brien

When Brian O'Brien played in the centre with Munster against Leinster at Lansdowne Road during the provincial championships of 1966 he made national headlines. Not because of his overall performance on that occasion but because of a freak accident, when he collided with one of his own players, that almost finished his career.

They're made of stern stuff down in the 'Parish', however, and the following season the Shannon three-quarter was back in action and terrorising the opposition with the crash-tackling style with which he had become synonymous.

Two years after the Lansdowne Road injury, Brian won his first cap for Ireland against France in Paris and he went on to win two more against England in Twickenham and against Scotland at Lansdowne Road. Although selected, a thigh strain forced him to cry off the Welsh game at the end of that season and that injury virtually put an end to his international career.

Brian O'Brien has been associated with the Shannon club for as long as he can remember. In 1959 while playing in a seven-a-side tournament, Brian suffered the first of what was to be a catalogue of rugby injuries when he broke his leg. It was a costly injury for the Shannon man, with his club going on without him to win the Munster Senior Cup for the first time in 1960.

By the early 1970s, Brian O'Brien had retired as a player but almost immediately devoted his time and efforts to coaching and administrative positions. Shannon benefited from his undoubted talents with memorable Munster Senior Cup victories over keen rivals, Garryowen, in 1977 and 1978, and went on to record a string of triumphs throughout the 1980s that elevated them to the highest echelons of Irish club rugby. As the glory and the years rolled on Brian O'Brien accepted the invitation to become club president of the Shannon club from 1986 until 1988 and it is significant that during that period the club won the league on two occasions as well as three consecutive Munster Cups, failing only narrowly to make it four-in-a-row in 1989.

As chairman of the Shannon selectors for the past two seasons, Brian has once again shown what a shrewd judge of the game he is and much of the credit for masterminding back-to-back successes has been pointed in his direction. A selector on the Munster team that beat the All-Blacks at Thomond Park in 1978, Brian also has the distinction of being an Irish selector when the Triple Crown was won in 1982; Irish representative on the Lions selection committee in 1983; and manager on a number of occasions of the Irish under-21 squad.

Employed by Moremiles Tyre Services in Limerick, Brian likes to relax in the Clare fishing village of Quilty and practise his pastimes of fishing and sub-aqua diving.

Married to the former Olive Bowyer, the couple have six children, singer/songwriter Siobhán and sons Brendan, Aidan, Ronan and Pádraig and youngest daughter, Maura.

"And don't forget my only grandson, Aran", Brian smiled.

> "Now that professionalism has been accepted in the game, I suppose we will have to live with it. But personally, I hope that it will not change the character of the game here in Limerick."

In conversation with Aidan Corr

Jim O'Brien

It was a warm day in May thirty years ago when Jim O'Brien thumbed a lift to the seaside in County Clare. As a student at the Shannon College of Hotel Management, he was new to the region and had crossed a great geographical landmark - the River Shannon - from his home in Wexford.

A car stopped and the driver was the legendary hotel manager, Jackie Donnelly, who proceeded to introduce the young O'Brien and his friends to the strange beauty of the Burren.

"We were going to Lahinch but Jackie hung a right through the Burren and we ended up eating ice creams in Lisdoonvarna," recalled the General Manager of Jurys, Limerick.

A summer job at Kelly's Hotel in his native Rosslare Strand was Jim O'Brien's introduction to the world of hotel management. "In a way I began my career by accident because Billy Kelly recommended that I attend the Shannon College," he said. There he made lasting friendships with other students including Peter Malone, now the MD of the Jurys' Group, and Liam Griffin of Griffin Hotels and trainer of the Wexford senior hurling team.

> "If I ask staff to be here at seven in the morning, bright and fresh and smiling, then I better be here myself. I would hope that I lead by example."

Like so many before him, O'Brien bunked down in the hostels at the base of Shannon Airport's control tower and was soon rubbing shoulders with the tourism pioneers of the region, including Brendan O'Regan and Jorgan Blum, the director of the Hotel College.

"I was lucky to have been in Shannon at the time," he said. "Because it was in this region that the tourist was given a unique experience of Ireland, where the tourist product was first identified and developed and the attitude was to look after the guests by exciting their minds."

After graduating from the Shannon College, Jim O'Brien spent some time in Germany, U.K. and the USA, where he took an associate degree in hotel management. In the Champagne region of France he found warm people and exciting times, but the lights of London attracted him and he worked at the famous London Tara before returning to the Clare Inn, Dromoland Castle Hotel and the Limerick Inn.

Jim O'Brien joined the Essco Collins company in Kilkishen for a short period, to grapple with graphs and learn about cash flow, profit projections and business plans. He worked in business then for eleven years.

Later he ran his own restaurant for three years with his wife, Helen and their daughters Orla and Ciara in Rosslare Strand.

Peter Malone persuaded him to return to Limerick for the third time. Jim O'Brien arrived to work in Jurys Hotel, just as the city was beginning to be transformed with an imaginative urban renewal programme. It coincided with a change in Jurys' marketing strategy, which saw a re-focus from American to more European visitors and a drive for the business customer.

As a hotelier, Jim O'Brien says the biggest problem is marketing the city and attracting people into Limerick. "Limerick is a stake holder in this hotel, as I am in the University or the waterways or the new City Hall. It is important that we all work together to get people into our city."

In conversation with Frank Hamilton

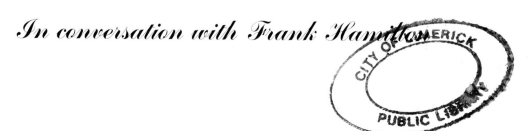

Loretta O'Brien

Loretta O'Brien *née* Larkin, was born in Finglas, Dublin on July 30th, 1951, birth sign, Leo. According to the astrologers this gives her a creative and communicative nature and a personality that lends itself to leadership and innovation. She lives with her husband, Ray, daughter Eimhear and son, Eoghan in Ardnacrusha, on the outskirts of Limerick City.

But why fabric patchwork as a medium of communication? She says she was bored; bored in Massachusetts, where she went with her husband, while he was on work transfer there in 1981. She had learned the skill of needlework from her mother, who was a tailoress and being in a centre of modern patchwork, New England, she adapted her earlier learning to this form of craftwork, "to fill my time". Janet Elwin was her first tutor and the first quilt she made was the *American Log Cabin* design.

Loretta brought her new-found expression, which she took to "like a fish to water" back home with her. Dyed fabrics became her paints and the sewing machine her brushes cum pallet. She involved herself in the Irish Patchwork Society and soon became a "mistress of the craft". In the Limerick area she began to teach. To further her teaching skills, she commuted to Belfast for a year, and took a diploma there in adult education.

> **"It is what can be achieved by adults when they return to learning that inspires me to contribute to their needs."**

She has become very involved in the Adult Resource Centre in the Kileely/Ballynanty area, where she teaches needlework and the City and Guilds classes in artistic creative fabric working.

Mainie Jellett, and the Russian artist, Kandinsky, are her favourite painters. Indeed, Loretta's designs echo Jellett's and Kandinsky's use of patterns and colours in some of her work. Ben Kiely and Brendan Kennelly are her favourite writers and Cliff Richard and Mícheál O Suilleabháin - her favourite musicians. The latter for his innovation and experimentation in the field of Irish music. Loretta's tastes are of a very Catholic nature indeed.

She was once described as having a "fiendish sense of humour" for her unique way of interpreting themes. When asked to do a wall hanging for Treaty 300 of the "Walls of Limerick", she made an intricate pattern of each step of the dance, *Fallaí Luimní* on a thirteen foot by two foot grey castellated cloth, instead of some heroic military display!

Loretta has exhibited her work both nationally and internationally, in places as far apart as Limerick and Lancaster, Austria and Ohio. She is currently the editor of the *Irish Patchwork Society Newsletter* and brought their annual conference, to Limerick in 1996. On this occasion she was also awarded the 1996 James Lawlor National Perpetual Trophy for Excellence in Patchworking.

This "Dub at the Stub" of creative expression and intricate craftwork in the Limerick area, has by her contribution become part of its ongoing and developing life, and will hopefully continue to do so for many a year to come.

In conversation with Donal O Murchu

Fr. Terence O'Brien

Fr. Terence O'Brien, an only child, was born in the heart of the city, just over Sarsfield Bridge, and is now parish priest in Limerick's rapidly growing suburb of Monaleen.

He was instrumental in establishing the Helpline switchboard at 25 Upper Cecil Street, where The Samaritans set up base. Not only that, but he had organised the bringing-together of a group of concerned citizens, who felt that with a changing social climate, there was more need than ever before to listen, reach out, and lighten the burden of those in distress.

The Limerick of the fifties was, in his own words, rather inward, where families kept to within their own circles.

"It wasn't a very pleasant place in which to live ... one half did not know how the other half lived, and problems were kept within family units. There were few social services available at the time, and, if you wanted help, there was really no place in which to go". An eleven-year sojourn in London, opened his eyes. In other words, he was made street-wise.

Shortly before he returned home in the late Bishop Murphy's era, he was struck by a billboard in the underground calling on the distressed to 'ring the Samaritans'.

"That simple message stuck in my mind. When I returned, to take up a teaching appointment at The Municipal Technical Institute (MTI), Limerick was undergoing something of an industrial revolution. While that was of benefit to city and county, in that it gave valuable employment, it also brought with it great social changes". From a few personal encounters with friends and personal acquaintances who were experiencing difficulty in coping with everyday life, that message of hope he had seen in the underground prompted him to tease out the possibilities of setting up the Samaritans in Limerick.

A meeting of influential citizens was called, chaired by the late Frank Lyddy, and addressed by RTE news reader, the late Charles Mitchel.

Shortly afterwards a steering committee was set up, headed by Pat Mortell. Upwards of seventy-five volunteers were trained, and 25 Upper Cecil Street became the listening ear for those in need of the service. That was in 1975.

> **"There will always be a need for the Samaritans in Limerick."**

Another milestone was reached a few years later, when The Samaritans spread their wings to Ennis, again initiated by him. Terence O'Brien initially served as assistant director in Limerick, and then director.

In the mid-eighties, he began to feel "burn-out", and felt it was time to stand down.

He concedes that although the problems which affect both young and old today have changed since the eighties, there is no replacement for personal contacts, despite ongoing technological advances. "The television is a poor replacement for the old tradition of visitations, and has led to greater isolation, especially in rural areas. The growing drug problem and increased unemployment have also contributed to a rise in the incidence of suicide, particularly amongst our young people and students."

On a different note, he is delighted with the structural changes in Limerick, a city, he says, which can now hold its head high with the best.

"Unlike when I was growing up, it is now a great place in which to live".

In conversation with John O'Shaughnessy

Cian O'Carroll

It is an Irish paradox of life that the man who was one of the key people involved in building Shannon Town from foundation stone to modern urban prosperity is not a native at all, but a Dublin import, born to Tipperary and Galway parents in Glasnevin. Cian O'Carroll came to Limerick thirty-six years ago and has done much to shape the physical environment in Limerick City and Shannon. Shannon Town Centre, The Granary and Workspace are examples of projects he initiated as head of property in Shannon Development from the mid 1960s.

A later job, twenty years on, saw Cian head up the Shannon Heritage and Banquets company with Shannon Development.

He retired this year with the quiet satisfaction of seeing a flourishing tourism trade attracted to Bunratty, Knappogue, Dun Guaire and King John's Castle as well as the Cliffs of Moher and Lough Gur. With his wife Ann's assistance, Cian who lives on Limerick's North Circular Road, has now established a consultancy practice concentrating on heritage tourism. Their two sons and two daughters are reared now, each one on the road.

Cian has deep interest in matters historical and makes the case strongly that if you live in a place, it is essential to know its context and history. He has written extensively for *The Other Clare*. As his contribution to Limerick Treaty 300 in 1991, he edited new editions of Dowd's and Lenihan's histories of Limerick. In early 1996 he undertook the research for a documentary broadcast on RTE Radio on the life of Catherine Hayes, the renowned nineteenth century Limerick soprano.

He mulls back over the genesis of Clare's second largest town and Ireland's first new town as if it was an awkward adolescent with curious ideas of its own about growing up.

> "Shannon town has grown from an empty area to one where 10,000 people share a community."

Cian O'Carroll remembers Shannon as a green and growing town, struggling to cope with the absence of kinship and continuity. "It was very different from other suburban areas, it had to be."

Shannon Heritage and Banquets is run on highly competitive lines and marketed internationally on the virtues of its originality and Irishness. "The music, the theatrical elements, the food have to excel and customer service is everything. In working on Shannon Town, I was dealing with the people on a professional basis. In this job I was meeting them in holiday mood. They had key expectations of being looked after, which had to be met."

A boost to being boss here was the privilege of meeting everyone: Raisa Gorbachov (charismatic), Mary Robinson (interested in everything), Japanese foreign ministers (ordered bacon and cabbage), the ambassadors and entertainers of the world. Nice work and he enjoyed it all while he had it. Now Cian O'Carroll is a young retiree with a commendable body of physically evident and abstract achievement behind him and there are bricks yet to stack.

"Limerick was a thousand years old when Shannon began and something of the same model had to be created within a compressed time scale. People of all nationalities came to the neighbourhood, connected only by the availability of work and housing close by other recently-arrived families."

In conversation with Rose Rushe

Pat O'Donnell

Pat O'Donnell, current President of the Limerick Leprechauns R.F.C., was destined to play rugby from the day he could walk, as his father Willie was an ardent supporter of Young Munsters.

It was only natural that Pat's early years saw him play in the famous 'black and amber' colours. He was subsequently approached to play for Presentation and played his first Munster Junior Cup Match at the tender age of fifteen.

Whilst with Presentation he won a Transfield Cup Medal and represented Munster at under 20 level, playing beside players like Colm Tucker, Michael McLoughlin and Billy Cronin. Pat's desire to play Senior Rugby saw him join Bohemians and for seventeen years Pat gave sterling and loyal service to a club with a proud tradition. I asked Pat to recall one memory of his playing days and without hesitation he referred to the Munster Senior Cup Final of 1980. Young Munsters beat Bohemians by the narrow margin of 9-7 on that day. Pat felt that during the game he had scored a perfectly good try but the referee disallowed it. Had it been given then he has no doubt that Bohemians would have been champions.

"What I enjoy most about Limerick Rugby is to experience the rivalry that exists between the clubs. The intensity at which the games are played has to be seen to be believed, but best of all the camaraderie after games where hostilities are buried, even if only temporarily, is second to none."

Pat's career in the motor trade began in Davin Motors on the Ennis Road. He continues to look after his customers from his own motor repair business to this day.

Pat married Mary Hickey in 1975 and they have two children, Rory and Deirdre.

Perhaps the medal cupboard might look bare but Pat has continued his love of rugby with the Limerick Leprechauns and in that company he has enriched the game by his contribution. The Limerick Leprechauns have over the years contributed in excess of £50,000 to local charities. It is Pat's ambition to improve on that figure over the next number of years.

The Leprechauns evolved from a team that was cobbled together by Larry Breen and Michael O'Flaherty to play against Garryowen F.C. in their centenary year. The geriatric brigade formed a secret pact with the lads from 'Tir na nÓg'.

The idea behind the Limerick Leprechauns was to provide an outlet for fun rugby for the more mature players, while also raising funds for local charities.

Under Pat's presidency the Limerick Leprechauns raised a considerable sum of money which was presented to The Samaritans, when in the season '95-'96 they played the famous Welsh touring side the 'Crawshay's'. It was the first time in years that an all Limerick side composed of 1st and 2nd Division players combined to take on a visiting team. For the record the locals were beaten comprehensively by the visitors.

Following on from the 'Crawshay's' game a decision was made that the Limerick Leprechauns should show the world what rugby in Limerick was all about. Combining this concept with the traditional idea of fundraising for charity, a trip to the U.S. evolved.

This was a momentous decision in the history of the Club and Pat hopes that its success will act as a catalyst for similar ventures in the future.

In conversation with Niall Cantrell

Tom and Helen O'Donnell

One of the country's longest-serving and best-loved politicians, Tom O'Donnell, and his wife Helen, a successful business woman in her own right and currently President of the Limerick Federation of Women's Organisations (LFWO), are very proud of both historical and modern day Limerick.

Tom, from a farming background in County Limerick and Helen, from a similar background in County Sligo, both with warm personalities, experienced no problems adapting to city life.

Helen, very involved in a number of worthwhile charitable organisations since coming to work in the city in the early 1980s, describes Limerick as "a vibrant, interesting and friendly place - a great place to live and work."

"Limerick people have a lot to be proud of and every reason to be confident" adds Helen, who showed that confidence when she opened her own restaurant, art gallery and craft centre in the city in 1993.

> **'For me Limerick is not only my home but the centre of my personal universe. To quote a line of one of my favourite songs: "I love those dear hearts and gentle people who live in my home town."'**
> **Tom O'Donnell**

keys and told him to take it for a spin. In his excitement, he overlooked that it was festooned with Fine Gael stickers and a loudspeaker appealing for votes for the Fine Gael candidate. On his return he was berated by his shocked colleagues for driving a Blueshirt car."

Both O'Donnells take an active interest in public affairs, especially the promotion of peace. Helen is a member of the National Forum for Peace and Reconciliation. Tom is currently chairman of the Peace Institute at the University of Limerick, the Centre of International Co-Operation, based at Shannon, the PAUL Partnership in Limerick, and the Limerick City and County Strategy Group.

Helen, the expert in the field, does the cooking in the O'Donnell household. However Tom admits to "giving a hand", but stories of smoke-filled kitchens in her absence suggest that household chores are best left to Helen.

Tom, elected to the Dáil for the first time in 1961 and the first Limerick man to be elected directly to the European Parliament, has many a story to tell from his years in active politics, which included four and a half years as a very successful Minister for the Gaeltacht.

Thinking back over those years, when he travelled up and down the country, he recalled a particular by-election encounter in the West of Ireland. "I arrived early one morning to a country polling station. A Fianna Fáil colleague in Europe approached and enquired about my new car. I handed him the car

The O'Donnells, who married in Rome in 1984, never considered their age difference a problem. "We have so much in common it was just never considered", explained the vivacious Helen.

An avid reader during his mobile political career, Tom still enjoys reading, and naturally, has a special interest in modern history and politics. Michael Collins is his hero. Helen enjoys an early morning swim before heading into the kitchen of her very busy Dolmen restaurant. They both share an interest in horses and like nothing more than a day or two at the races, when time permits.

In conversation with Dymphna Bracken

Sean O'Grady

For ten years Seán O'Grady worked out in the garage of his home after a car crash left him disabled. His efforts were rewarded with a bronze medal for discus in the 1996 Paralympic Games. A well-known hurler in his younger days with Old Christians and the Limerick minor team, he was determined that disability would not prevent him taking part in competitive sport.

Today he is nationally recognised as Ireland's Atlanta Games bronze medalist, an articulate and charming spokesman for his sport. President Robinson appointed him to the Council of State shortly after a victorious home-coming.

Seán O'Grady sees the honour and indeed the bronze medal, not so much for himself but a tribute to all those people "in the background, who helped me to compete at the highest level. It is a medal for everybody, it makes my whole sporting career worthwhile."

"I was so engrossed in sport before the accident that it was a natural progression that I would want to continue it in some way."

A CBS Sexton Street boy, he was steeped in sport in the carefree days when he and his blonde wife Cecilia, affectionately known to family and friends as Cecil, were involved in Old Christians G.A.A. Club. Seán and his wife, their two teenage children, Alan (14) and Aileen (11) are a close knit unit surrounded by supportive family and a wide circle of friends. And now Seán is a leading official in Irish Wheelchair Associate Sport.

"When I came out of hospital I was introduced to the Irish Wheelchair Association sports section and met a great friend in Michael Cunningham. I learned later that he won a gold medal in Canada in 1976 throwing the javelin."

In 1987 he met Bantry man, Seanie McGrath, a PE student in the University of Limerick. "He is an amputee swimmer and I knew he was going to qualify for Seoul. I had a chat with Seanie and he agreed to coach me. That year I got my first cap for Ireland in the Stoke Manderville Games in the UK. My throwing distances started to improve and I was selected for Seoul and that was the icing on the cake."

Trips to the World Championships in Holland and the Paralympics in Barcelona followed.

Conscious that he required some professional advice, Seán approached local teacher Declan O'Donoghue who is one of the best throws coaches in the country.

In 1994 at the World Athletic Championships in Berlin, Seán took a silver medal in the shot-putt and also in the discus. Later he won gold and silver in the 1995 World Games in Stoke Mandeville, and from then his sights were set on Atlanta.

Throughout the winter Sean practiced indoor at Bawnmore and he feels that this all year regime improved his distances in the Spring.

"We always gear my training on an able-bodied thrower. Obviously there are things that I cannot do but all the upper body strength and power training, push ups, sit ups and all the work is based on an able bodied thrower."

The rest as they say is history. He is quick to point out however that the Irish Paralympic Team brought back ten medals.

In conversation with Frank Hamilton

Bill O'Keeffe

William O'Keeffe went into Limerick Prison as temporary staff for the summer of 1960 and remained there for thirty-five years, rising along the way to the rank of Prison Governor.

Better known as Bill, "all my relatives call me Liam", he is a native of Athenry, County Galway, where he was born in 1936. He has one brother, Dixie, who was ordained to the priesthood in 1959 and now lives in Arizona, U.S.A.

Bill attended national school in Athenry and St. Jarlath's College, Tuam, where he played football and hurling in the Connacht Colleges' Championships. His senior school days were spent in St. Senan's Secondary School, Killaloe, County Clare, to where his father was transferred as a Garda. He continued his hurling with Killaloe, "The happiest days of my life were spent there, where I met my wife, Phil, from Bridgetown".

After school, Bill went to work as an invoice clerk with R. & J. O'Dwyer, Gerald Griffin St., Limerick, until he joined the prison service. "I was there temporary and intended only staying for the holidays, but the wages were better and I agreed to stay for a while".

He got married in 1963 to Phil. They have three children, Noreen, Catherine and Thomas. He was now fully committed to the service. All training at the time was "on the job". He worked his way through the disciplinary and clerical grades to assistant governor, deputy governor, and he became

"People complain that prisoners have a great time in prison, but I don't go along with that. They are deprived of their freedom, but they must be fed and looked after physically and mentally and be treated as human beings."

governor in 1985. He retired ten years later, on 23 June, 1995.

Recalled Bill: "the Limerick Prison I joined and the Limerick Prison I left were two different prisons. In the early days it was like an old folks home dealing with local prisoners. The numbers were smaller, but there was a dramatic change in the mid 70s when it became a top security prison".

"The Prison Service was very good to me. I enjoyed my job and I liked helping prisoners where I could. There was a tremendous staff in Limerick.

"While I was there I never felt pressure, but since I came out I realise now there must have been pressure. The staff and myself had our differences, but the job was always the winner".

He states firmly that there is no crisis in the prison service itself, but there is a shortage of prison spaces for prisoners. "If there were sufficient places and prisoners spent their full term as imposed by the courts, that would be more of a deterrent against committing crime. I have found myself that people who serve their full sentences very rarely return, especially those who served long sentences."

His greatest challenge these days is working on his golf handicap. "I do a bit of gardening and if I don't play golf, I walk every day for four miles. I could have stayed at work for another five years, but I had given all I could to the service. I wanted to enjoy the rest of my life with my wife now that my family is reared".

In conversation with Brian McLaughlin

Eddie O'Neill

Maybe it's because he's a twin that Eddie O'Neill lives his life at twice the pace of everyone else, and why he led a double life for most of twenty-five years.

By day he was a central-heating salesman with the ESB but by night he was the singing butler at the Bunratty Castle medieval banquet.

Soldier, draughtsman, salesman, singer and actor, Eddie has done it all, and in retirement the pace has hardly slackened for one half of a set of twins born to a taxi driver and his dressmaker wife at Thomas Street in the heart of Limerick City in 1923.

His mother was "a total extrovert", so he blames the lure of the stage and his passion for performing on her. While attending Sexton Street CBS, he was a soloist boy soprano at St. John's Cathedral, and after an "Emergency" wartime stint in the army alongside his twin Jimmy, Eddie came back into civilian life as a draughtsman with the ESB and in the 1950s and 1960s was starring with the Cecilians Musical Society.

He excelled in flamboyant romantic roles like *The White Horse Inn* and *The Merry Widow,* so it was natural that he took more than a casual interest when he brought a group to the three-years-established Bunratty Castle feast.

"A few days later I was passing Bunratty in the course of my job, called in and asked to speak to the Manager, Christy Lynch. I told him that I thought the 'page' character in the banquet performance lacked

"She made me feel seven feet tall every day of my life"; Eddie O'Neill speaking of Irene, who became his wife and mother of their five children.

authority. I was handed a script and three nights later I was on." It was October 1966, and Eddie was to fill the doublet and hose of the castle butler for twenty-three years until he was sixty-eight years old.

He may not have been king but he ruled the castle. His *Little Bridget Flynn* solo was a masterpiece of tongue-in-cheek coyness and if his "My Lords and Ladies" failed to command order, he could silence an over-exuberant table of revellers with a withering stare and the encore - "My Lords and Ladies ... and Peasants."

He had married a childhood friend, even though he and Irene did not see each other for an interval of twenty years, and she is still the great love of his life more than twenty years after her death from cancer in 1974.

With four daughters and a son to look after, Eddie continued in his dual roles but after six years alone, romance came back into his life on the drawbridge at Bunratty when he welcomed Joy from California. "There was a spark straight away" Eddie recalls, and a year later on June 21st, they were on honeymoon in Paris. It was Joy who taught him machine embroidery, and even after she died in 1988, Eddie continued to make embroidered Irish dancing costumes, Mass vestments and banners.

In an exceptionally full life "Bunratty was the most wonderful time of all" says Eddie who intoned the castle's farewell to its guests -" the bridge is down between the real and the fantasy" ... for the last time in 1989.

In conversation with Dermot Walsh

Margaret O'Shaughnessy

Margaret O'Shaughnessy is a high flyer - maybe not in the literal sense - but her aspiration for Foynes Flying Boat Museum is to make it one of the country's top tourist attractions.

Dynamic, energetic and always on the move, Margaret is devoted to Foynes on the Shannon Estuary and her every waking hour is spent dreaming up ideas that will put the historic flying boat port firmly on the tourist map. "In the 30s you could come to Foynes by land, sea, rail and air", she recounted. Irish coffee originated in Foynes, invented by Joe Sheridan in 1947, to warm up the cold and weary transatlantic traveller and naturally Margaret is now getting mileage out of that with a very successful Irish coffee-making world championship.

Involved with the Flying Boat Museum since its infancy over seven years ago, she saw it rise from a refurbished building to what it is now; a unique tourist product.

"Indefatigable in her battle to have Foynes recognised and its place in aviation history assured for all times, she is a dedicated trail blazer, who truly merits our admiration and acclaim."
Trail Blazers of Ireland.

She and her committee landed a star, none other than the household name Irish actress, Maureen O'Hara, whose husband, Captain Charles Blair, flew the last flying-boat out of Foynes in 1945.

Today Maureen O'Hara still takes a keen interest in the affairs of the museum as its patron. The American connection continued when consultants from California were brought in to draw up plans for an extended museum. This is a one million pound project with an exciting new attraction, which will allow the visitor to experience a simulated computer trip by flying-boat from Foynes to New York.

Museum Curator, Margaret, is keeping her fingers crossed that the funds will be forthcoming, and points out that the new computer simulator will allow fear of flying courses "which are big business in England".

Another initiative of the museum is the completion of the history of aviation at Foynes. "Flying boats are brought into the harbour periodically so that the younger generation can come to understand what they are and see what they are about", said Margaret.

She is acutely aware that to draw visitors and tourists to the Shannon Estuary, people will have to be made aware of its existence and the amenities it has to offer.

Born in London, but brought to Foynes at ten months, Margaret has no problem about revealing her age of forty-two. She was employed by the Bank of Ireland at various branches and married her husband, Tom, who works at Foynes harbour, in 1975.

She is the only woman, so far, to be honoured by the Trail Blazers of Ireland, when in 1994 she was awarded their diploma of honour. The citation reads: "In pursuing her dream of an aviation museum in Foynes, she demonstrated courage, dynamism and persistence of effort on an heroic scale as she fought to honour the brave pilots and crews and vitally important ancillary services who took part in the fundamentally important proving flights, and those who turned the dream of scheduled transatlantic passenger flights through Foynes into reality in 1939.

In conversation with Brian McLaughlin

Mary O'Sullivan

Mary O'Sullivan, from Askeaton has suffered with recurring cancer problems for the past ten years.

Before being diagnosed with the disease, she had the trauma of dealing with a malfunctioning kidney and had undergone a hysterectomy.

"The last ten years have been very difficult" admits this lovely, sympathetic, kind and gentle woman.

In spite of being in constant pain, Mary set up a cancer support group with two friends, Linda Leonard and Anne O'Donnell, five years ago. The group meets each Wednesday for morning tea or coffee, at the Limerick Social Services Centre, in Henry Street.

"I found that while I was in hospital, the counselling and support was great, but when I was discharged, few people would talk to me about cancer.

Mary recently organised a counselling room, next to the oncology clinic at Limerick's Regional Hospital, where people who have either just been diagnosed with cancer or are worried about going through treatment, can come and have a chat with herself or any one of the support group.

"It's amazing how people react to having someone who has gone through the trauma of cancer and its treatment share their feelings. They find it very comforting."

"Some just want to talk their feelings out, others just want to sit and cry, and that's also very good for them."

Ten years ago, Mary's beloved mother died from lung cancer at the early age of fifty-eight and Mary went through a deep and traumatic grief.

"We were very close and her death hit me very hard. Towards the end of the year after her death, I was feeling very run down and had very bad headaches. The doctors admitted me to hospital with meningococcal meningitis."

"While I was there, a routine examination showed a lump on my breast. The doctors did a biopsy and when the result came back malignant, I was devastated. I didn't know much about cancer at the time and thought it was a death sentence. I cried and cried, wondering how Jim, my husband, and my three children, Barry, Sinéad and John would cope without me. Jim was wonderful, holding my hand and reassuring me that cancer of the breast was cured all the time."

Mary had to wait for five weeks, until her meningitis cleared up, to have her breast removed. She's since lost her second breast to the disease.

Two years ago, ten lumps appeared along the scar tissue of the breast; they were all malignant; she's recently had a malignant lump removed from her neck; has to use a special pump for five hours every day to relieve a build up of fluid in her lymph glands; and attends a special clinic in Cork to cope with the pain.

Over forty people come to the weekly coffee mornings for a cup of tea or coffee and a chat.

"We have people from all walks of life, both men and women. They find the weekly contact with others great and we all have each other's phone numbers, so help, advice and consolation is always at hand if anyone needs it."

"Every day I have a chat with God and tell him, that if he wants me to continue my voluntary work in helping people to come to terms with cancer, he has to leave me here."

In conversation with Valerie Sweeney

Sister Imelda O'Sullivan

Sister Imelda O'Sullivan spends her life "trying to empower the people to appreciate their roots".

She points out that unemployment is a huge problem in Moyross, the Limerick City housing estate where she works. "It's running at 70.6% at present and if FÁS wasn't there, it would be 80%." She tries to get across the dignity of work and suggests that unemployment does not help family life.

She adds: "People on training courses and community education get up in the morning and its good for the children to see this. We need a ritual for life, whether its part-time work, community education or being involved in a voluntary capacity - it gives people dignity while unemployment isolates people".

A native of Ballylickey, near Bantry, in West Cork, Sister Imelda is a member of the Little Sisters of the Assumption and is one of twelve children. She trained as a nurse in the Mater Hospital in Dublin and graduated in Social Studies in Cardiff.

Youth work is her first love and she worked in this capacity in Cardiff, Galway and North Clare before coming to Limerick.

Sitting in the uncluttered sittingroom of her semi-detached home in Moyross, she points out that she has been in the area for six years. In her first twelve months, through her involvement with adult education, she discovered that there are a lot of talented and gifted people in Moyross. "But because they live in Moyross, they didn't have any avenue or venue to display their giftedness and I was determined to use the media to highlight some of their abilities."

> **"Adult education has made a positive contribution to people's lives by giving them self-esteem and confidence. It provides an opportunity of second chance education and is a means of making friends."**

The Moyross Environment Movement of Residents Yearly campaign has provided a joint forum for joint action with the Cleansing Department, the Parks Section of Limerick Corporation and the local people. It has also encouraged better partnership with the County Council for three parks which are outside the city.

"Through M.E.M.O.R.Y. the children are rewarded for their efforts by having leisure activities provided for them. They are also learning, through the art competitions organised, what their role is in the environment."

"The need for funds was always a major problem in Moyross as every activity requires money which was not readily available. In an effort to replace the local community mini-bus, I sought support from the religious in Limerick and within a month had £2,000 for the bus. With support from friends like Fr. Paddy Tyrell S.J., we got additional money to pay for the bus which is used by local families, charity organisations, football teams, adult education groups and so on. It is now self-financing."

"Jim Kemmy, when he was mayor, and Mary Lawless, also helped to raise large sums of money for the community."

It was during a sabbatical that Sister Imelda decided she wanted to live close to people on the margins of society and she now feels at home in Moyross - a real compliment coming from a West Cork woman!

Her dream for Moyross - "that people discover their own resources and begin to set up structures of a self-help nature which would be financially supporting. The only way to build a society where each one is valued and respected is by everyone working together."

In conversation with Brian McLaughlin

Senator Jan O'Sullivan

The city's first female Labour Mayor, co-founder of a political party, mother and former teacher, Senator Jan O'Sullivan feels the city's new self confidence will contribute to its future commercial and cultural development well into the next century.

Born into a literary background on the outskirts of the city, in County Clare, her late father, Ted Gale, was a journalist and her mother, Pat, still active in the local community, was a teacher. One of a family of two, Jan followed in her mother's footsteps and on obtaining a degree in English and French from Trinity College, she returned to Villiers, her alma mater.

Life took an exciting turn for Jan in the seventies when she met and married local doctor, Paul O'Sullivan, and moved to Canada.

"It was an exciting time in Canada and we met and made friends with many different kinds of people".

Jan admits to getting her first taste for politics through the co-operative movement in Canada.

On the birth of their daughter Emily, currently a student at Dublin's Kevin Street College of Technology, the O'Sullivans decided to return home.

On their return , Jan opened her own Montessori pre-school and became involved in the Limerick Women's Collective.

"Children are supposed to be born equal, but they do not all get the same chances. I was impressed with Deputy Jim Kemmy's political ideals", admitted Jan. She co-founded the Democratic Socialist party with the Deputy. It later merged with the Labour party.

"One of my dearest wishes would be to see people swimming and bathing in clear unpolluted Shannon waters within the city before I am too old and stiff to join them."

Her first election success was in 1985, when along with Win Harrington she was one of two women elected to the City Council. Her contribution to local politics was recognised in 1993, when she was elected Mayor, only the third female mayor of the city in almost 800 years. "It was a great honour and a privilege to be representing the people as their first citizen".

Elected a Senator, following the 1993 general election, Jan favours the quota system to encourage more women to get involved. "Politics would benefit from more involvement by women and I think waiting for equal representation to happen naturally will take too long" she added.

Jan, who has visited Northern Ireland on a number of occasions as a member of the Forum for Peace and Reconciliation, recalls a lighter moment of sitting between De Valera's grandson, Éamon O'Cuiv, and a Loyalist ex-prisoner from the Shankill Road, and not been able "to get a word in edge ways". "When people relate to each other as human beings, there is hope for the future."

She believes that the physical improvements over the last ten years have given Limerick "more confidence" - a confidence which has been strengthened by ties with the university. As chairperson of the twenty-year-old Limerick-Quimper Twinning Committee, she is also active in developing links overseas, believing this to be "vital for any modern city".

A member of the Regional Authority, Senator O'Sullivan is always to the forefront on environmental issues. "I think that plans to make the Shannon a pollution-free river will have huge potential for both industrial and tourism development."

In conversation with Dymphna Bracken

Mícheal O Suilleabhain and Nóirín Ní Riain

Nóirín Ní Riain is a county Limerick woman and very proud of it! "I was conceived in Lough Gur - one of the earliest sites of human habitation in Ireland - born in Limerick City, and raised in Caherconlish, only six miles from Glenstal Abbey, which was to become so important in my musical journey".

And what a journey that has been up to now. Nóirín has established herself as a carrier of spiritual songs from many cultures. Her trilogies of recordings during the 1980s with the Benedictine monks of Glenstal Abbey are regarded as international classics at this stage. Since then she has moved on to a solo career that has taken her from India to Brazil, from China to Canada.

"One of my most treasured memories was singing for the Dalai Lama at an international peace gathering in Costa Rica. What also comes back to me was the power of singing the songs of Mirabai, the sixteenth century Rajasthani saint, during a tour of India last year with Mick.

Mick turns out to be no less than Mícheál O Súilleabháin, Ireland's famed pianist, composer, and professor of Music at the University of Limerick.

"Nóirín and I met as students on our first day in the Music Department of University College Cork. At that stage neither of us had warmed to Irish and we were Nóirín Ryan and Michael O'Sullivan (from Clonmel, County Tipperary). But in Cork my name was automatically translated through the strong local culture into Mick Sullivan. And Mick Sullivan I have always been for Nóirín - although she does have a sort of copyright on the name. Others should beware of using it too liberally!"

Mícheál's laughter is infectious, and Nóirín relishes his humour with a wry smile.

> They both obviously take a wicked delight in coming across people who know their music but do not know they are married. It seems to vindicate their sensitivity to the professional independence of each other's musical voice.

"I'm famous at this stage for saying in the most public way that Mick is perfect. Of course he's not, but I'm obviously more than a bit batty about him! We have the most amazing time together, which is only heightened now when concerts and other commitments drag us away from one another".

Mícheál's commitments at the postgraduate Irish World Music Centre, which he set up at the University of Limerick in January 1994, are ones that he finds stimulating.

"I really love the atmosphere here. I am surrounded by wonderfully creative students and colleagues who share with me the excitement of witnessing the growth of new music and dance programmes at the Irish World Music Centre. I also find an increasing connection between my own personal musical search and my educational work at the University of Limerick".

Nóirín and Mícheál are very careful to respect the line between their professional lives and their personal relationship.

Respecting the individuality of each other's music is something they aspire to not only in their musical lives, but also in their personal relationship.

For Mícheál and Nóirín, the story of their music is the story of themselves. For Nóirín, the voice is everything, the fingerprint of her soul. For Mícheál, the piano is the medium for his most intimate expressions. Together they work their way through life, always leaning towards the constantly changing spiritual balance within themselves and within their friendship.

Perhaps you must know the music of one to understand the other. Let you the listener decide.

In conversation with Eleanor Plunkett

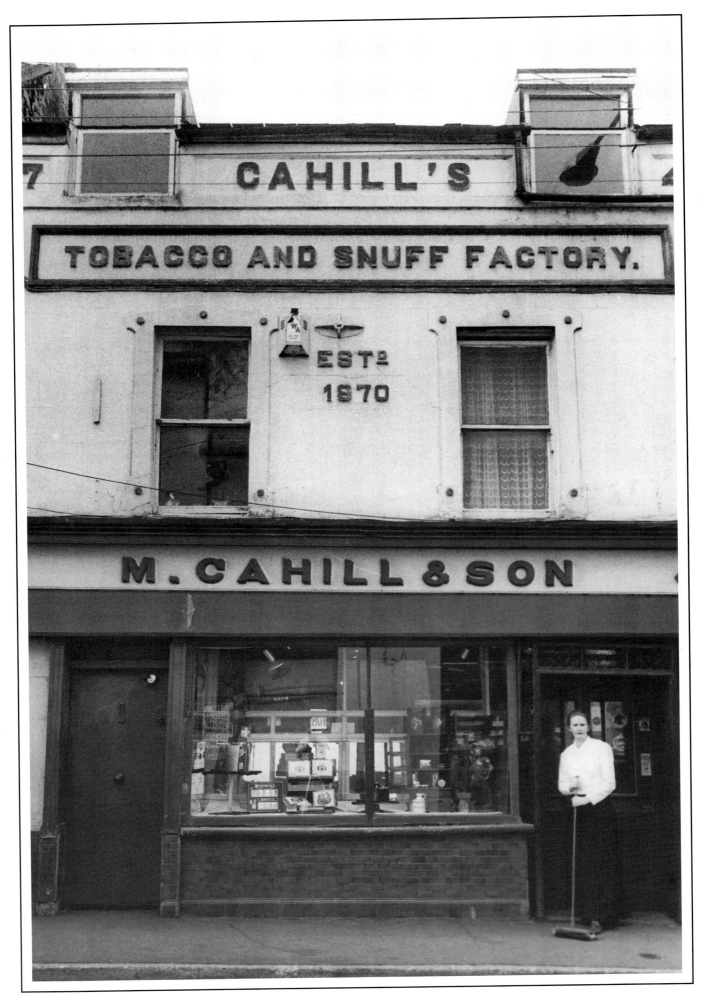

Eleanor Purcell

Cahill's Tobacconist of Wickham Street is a mecca for the Mid-West's pipe smokers. The only tobacco shop between Cork and Dublin, Cahill's has been loyally serving its customers for over one-hundred-and-twenty-five years.

The owner, Eleanor Purcell, proudly reveals that "people travel miles to buy our tobacco."

The shop has been part of the Purcell family for two generations. Jim Purcell, Eleanor's father, worked in Cahill's as an apprentice, met his future wife there and finally bought it off the Cahills in 1961.

Eleanor has fond memories of her childhood in the shop. "As soon as we could see over the counter we worked there. My father was very popular, a very nice man. There was a very strong ethos of serving the customer."

Cahill's doesn't have to recreate traditional shopkeeping values because it has never lost them. Step in the door and you find yourself on the threshold of history. Among the cluttered wooden shelves and shining glass cases lie all kinds of smoking paraphernalia. Cartons of cigars and parcels of loose tobacco bear exotic and revered names like Duma, Tobajara, King Edwards and Afton. Tobacco pouches and knives and snuff boxes peer out from every corner. The shop's crowning glory is its collection of pipes of every shape and size, which stand out for inspection around the walls of the shop. Add in the worn linoleum floor covering, the long wooden counter, the old style weighing scales and finally the wafting smell of tobacco and snuff and the turn-of-the-century ambience is completed. Top it off with individual attention to each customer and it is easy to see why Eleanor is so enchanted with the character of the shop.

Looking slightly out of place, but providing interesting contrast, shiny new zippos and hip flasks have joined the wares of Cahill's in recent years. The gaudy blue Lotto machine in the corner is another concession to modernisation.

"We're on to our sixth generation of customers. We're the last remnant of what was an important industry in Limerick and the last remnant of a time when people were shopkeepers."

However, despite her love for her father's trade, it came as a surprise to her when she was the one chosen to follow in his footsteps. Having completed a degree in social studies in Trinity she returned to Limerick when her father died. "I didn't have another job so it fell to me to work in the shop. I originally planned to keep it for two years and then sell it but I began to see I liked it."

Eleanor now lives in Adare where she also runs a very successful crafts shop called Black Abbey Crafts.

Eleanor, who smokes herself, sees tobacco as a declining trade rather than a dying trade. Freely admitting that cigarette smoking is not good, she would prefer to see the emphasis on the humble pipe.

"Pipe smoking is a relaxing practice which leaves time for contemplation. In moderation, I would see it as life-enriching."

In her few moments of spare time, she enjoys gardening, horseriding, animals and the countryside.

In conversation with Brian Quinlivan

Bernard & Brian Quinn

"Many men have been capable of doing a wise thing, more a cunning thing, but very few a generous thing".

So said one Jonathan Swift many years ago.

Mr. Swift would surely salute the brothers Bernard and Brian Quinn from St. Enda's House on the Roxboro Road for their generosity towards the people of the torn and tattered former Yugoslavia.

Always an interested political observer, Bernard, like many others, was shocked by the unfolding events in Bosnia and Croatia after the division of the former Yugoslavia in April 1992.

In September 1993, Bernard was on a tour of duty in Dublin's Cherry Orchard Refugee Centre as a member of Limerick City Civil Defence. He was privately shown, by the refugees, a video that would change his and Brian's lives irreversibly.

Bernard sat amidst silent tears and anguish as the screen showed eerie scenes of devastated towns and villages and mutilated corpses of men, women and children littering the streets.

On his return to Limerick, Bernard, his brother Brian and others set up Friends of Bosnia; a humanitarian aid organisation.

Many in Ireland gave generously when they saw the horrors of ethnic cleansing taking place in the heart of 'civilised' Europe, but Bernard, Brian and Friends went one better.

They guaranteed that the aid would get to where it was most needed, by taking it there themselves.

By the time Friends of Bosnia made it through to Mostar in early November 1993, the besieged Moslems were being attacked by Bosnian Serbs on one side and their former Croat allies on the other.

The Limerick men came to feed women and children who had begun to eat grass and snakes to survive.

The Quinn brothers can tell of many horrors, having now completed five humanitarian trips to Bosnia, but perhaps the most blood-chilling is an account they received of extremist Bosnian and Chetnik Serbs lining up children and slitting their throats. Their only crime: they were Moslems.

This sort of "ethnic cleansing" was going on all around as Bernard and Brian, and a few others, tried to bring some help to these tortured people. Away from the heartache and life-threatening situations of their aid trips, brothers Brian and Bernard still have their day jobs. Bernard works as a guillotine operator for a Shannon-based company while Brian looks after the mentally and physically handicapped.

> **What drives Bernard and Brian is an inability to say "that's dreadful" and simply change the channel.**

Friends of Bosnia is based at the Quinns' home, St. Enda's House, on the Roxboro Road, and has become a family affair.

Their mother, Catherine, brothers, Con, Gerard, Colm and Paul, and sisters, Mary, Noelle and Antoinette all help out with the storage and office work.

The brothers would not live anywhere but in Limerick. They are delighted with the generosity of the people, and proud of the beauty of their native city.

"When we bring Bosnian refugees to Limerick," Bernard says, "they all remark on how beautiful it is. They are seeing the new Limerick. And, perhaps they are thinking of their own cities - which will be beautiful again too."

In conversation with Trish O'Dea

Ted Russell

A prophet in his own time is the exception rather than the rule. This paraphrasing of the words of St. Matthew was used in reference to George Edward (Ted) Russell by the then Minister for Defence and the Marine, David Andrews. The occasion was when the Minister officially re-named Limerick Dock as the Ted Russell Dock in 1993. The Minister, although of a different political party, described Ted Russell as "one of Limerick's outstanding public figures".

It has been said that he was the only person, other than the present Queen of England, who has had a city docks named after him during his lifetime. The tribute is understandable, for Ted Russell joined the Board of the Limerick Harbour Commissioners in 1946, the year the present Harbours Act came into being. He had been chairman from 1966 until he retired in 1992, and is still a member today, fifty years on.

He was also Mayor of Limerick five times, having served on the City Council for thirty-seven years until he retired in 1979. It was in 1957, when on an official visit to the United States, that the former mayor recounted one of the most embarrassing incidents of his life. "The great chain of office, worn by the mayor on special occasions, went missing for almost 12 hours", he recalled. "After a sleepless night and endless prayers for its recovery, it turned up just in time on unlocking the boot of our official car!", he explained with relief.

Ted, who was born in 1912, the week the *Titanic* sank, acknowledges that it was not until June of 1995 that he received his greatest honour. In recognition of his long service to the city of his birth, he was made an Honorary Freeman of Limerick. Only fifty-seven people had been given this distinction since 1877.

His career as a Dáil deputy, to use his own words, was "short and sharp". It lasted just one term, 1957 - 1961, as an Independent, although he had been a member of Clann na Poblachta party previously, and stood unsuccessfully for them on three occasions.

Ted Russell served for eight distinguished years as a member of Seanad Éireann. His family background was Parnellite and Cumann na nGael. Looking back on those years and his time in the Oireachtas, he said "I have mixed feelings about it now. It was interesting, but it was very much a full-time job. I had a lot of business responsibilities at the time, and quite honestly, I always preferred local politics".

Despite all his years of public activity, which included getting a Final Irish Rugby Trial in 1938, it is his work with the Cancer Association of Ireland that is the most significant for Ted Russell. As its Chairman from 1949 to 1961, he saw the building of Dublin's St. Luke's Hospital and St. Agatha's Treatment Centre in Cork, as well as a number of diagnostic clinics throughout the country. In 1972, this Freeman presented to the Corporation a parcel of land, at Barrington's Pier, which has now been developed into one of the most beautiful parks in his native city.

Married to Derry (*née* Gleeson), originally from Nenagh, for almost fifty years now, the Russells have three daughters and one son.

> "I always believe that the more fortunate you have been in life, the greater your obligation is to contribute to the welfare and happiness of the less fortunate in our society."

In conversation with Arthur Quinlan

Eamon Ryan

Having given his adopted city a heart transplant as the man who assembled the properties for Limerick's urban renewal transformation, Eamon Ryan is now injecting new vigour and energy into the city's business as head of the Limerick City Enterprise Board.

This son of a Pallas Green fuel merchant has an inside track on the partnership between the State and the private sector. In charge of property at Limerick Corporation, he was centrally involved with the development team in giving the lead in the £300 million revitalisation of the city's worn-out heart.

Having a frontline role in the urban renewal initiative not only sharpened up his know-how and insights on business dealings, it also developed a network of contacts within the world of business, which is a key asset in the job at the Enterprise Board, where he has been chief executive since 1993.

Eamon was also picked to spearhead other major developments, including the facelift for the Galvone Industrial Estate and the development of an eighteen-hole municipal golf course at Rathbane, which opens for play in 1997. All of this brought him into constant contact and co-ordinated effort with the Shannon Development regional agency, as well as other State, business, financial and legal bodies.

"Shannon Development has a very wide brief as the regional economic development agency, so there was a need for a body which would focus exclusively on the city in fostering new enterprise and new ideas on enterprise", he says. And while he heads up an open-door operation which tries to cut red tape to the minimum for those wanting to get into business or into bigger business, he is particularly cheered by the

quality of the ventures coming on stream and also by the low degree of failure among the enterprises that his board has backed.

Eamon Ryan is proud that the annual "Enterprising Limerick" exhibition, organised by the Board, provides a showcase each year for over fifty businesses in the city. He is also happy that half of the proposals which have been helped by the board have come from the unemployed. And while those helped are largely in the thirty to forty-five year age group, the Enterprise Board is also looking to the future with initiatives directed at schools of primary and secondary levels.

"I don't do things by halves"; the approach which Eamon Ryan has brought to his job as Chief Executive of the Limerick City Enterprise Board.

The Limerick City Enterprise Board has joined with its county counterpart to set up one of six PLATO (small business development) schemes in the country, under which multinational firms assign top executives to provide guidance for small firms. "We are fortunate to have such a strong base of overseas firms in the city and county, which helped us meet the conditions for involvement.

Schooled at the CBS in Tipperary, Eamon joined the Mid-Western Health Board from school before being promoted to Limerick Corporation in 1981. He married another local government official, Wendy, who is now a partner in Murphy Ryan and Associates, Human Resources and Management consultants. They have three daughters and one son. One of the reasons why Eamon was handed the task of setting up the new Limerick municipal golf course was his own involvement with the game. He has been golfing for sixteen years and until the new Rathbane course comes on stream, his driving force in leisure time is spent on the courses at Lahinch and Tipperary.

In conversation with Dermot Walsh

Tom Ryan

"I'm a painter in the classical tradition, a practitioner of taste, talent and technique". The talent is God-given, the technique learned in the classrooms of Limerick and Dublin, moulded and guided by a Yorkshire man called Richard Butcher and the great Sean Keating, a fellow Limerickman.

Tom Ryan is entirely without modesty where his talent is concerned but endearingly, he's also unaffected by artistic snobbery. He brought his work to the masses in community halls across North Dublin and other parts of the country, and the people responded with their applause and cheque books.

Born in St. Joseph's Street in Limerick in 1929, the son of Tipperary-born parents, Tom Ryan is as matter of fact about his childhood as he is about his artistic talent.

There was no artistic talent in the family, but when they moved to Davis Street at the onset of war in 1939, Tom became a pupil in Sexton Street C.B.S.

A Christian brother spotted the boy of "unusual talent" and persuaded his parents to send him to the School of Art, where Richard Butcher instilled a regard for tradition and technique that has brought Ryan fame, but also kept him outside the Pale of Ireland's evolving art world of the last thirty years.

But for Ryan, surviving on seven shillings-and-six pence a week pocket money, painting was his life. From college it was back to his roots in the Limerick School of Art to a job without tenure or prospects. "And it was then the trouble began" he says, explaining how the promotion of the modernists isolated his mentor Keating and Ryan himself by association.

Salvation for Tom Ryan was a conviction in that God-given talent and the ordinary people who remained untouched by the internal wars of artistic politics.

Perhaps it is as a portrait painter that Ryan has achieved his greatest success. Presidents, cardinals and politicians have been captured by Ryan's brush, including the late Jeremiah Newman and Éamon de Valera.

He lives in Ashbourne in County Meath, a stone's throw from Dublin and the walls of his spacious studio are adorned by his work. Canvasses pile up in corners. His six children, four sons and two daughters and his wife, Mary, have been painted again and again.

Now in his mid-sixties he dismisses any tentative inquiry about retirement.

"I never got a halfpenny from any institution" Ryan says, displaying a cynicism about the influencers of Art, "and neither did anyone of my tradition."

Accolades have come his way. President of the Royal Hibernian Academy for ten years, he brought the Gallagher Gallery in Ely Place to fruition. He's an honorary member of the Royal Academy London and the Royal Scottish Academy and associated with the National College of Art and Design, The British School at Rome, a founder member of the European Council of National Academies of Fine Art and the recipient of a Doctor of Letters from the University of Limerick. Tom Ryan designed the one pound coin and the Millenium fifty pence piece and the list of associations and involvements goes on.

None of his six children has inherited his talent. Ryan seems glad. "It is too difficult, you need talent and you need it in a variety of forms" he says. There are no days off.

Tom Ryan remains defiantly committed to being a painter in the classical tradition.

In conversation with Mary Wilson

Mainchín Seoighe

For a great many people, the name of Mainchín Seoighe is inseparable from their sense of what Limerick really is. Through his ten books and other writings, his lectures and his weekly column in the *Limerick Leader,* he has opened up a door into Limerick's past for his audience, building on their sense of place, rooting it in history and bringing it to life with his stories of characters, events and legends. Generous to a fault in sharing his considerable knowledge, there is hardly a village or town in the county where he has not lectured in his time.

Not surprisingly, Mainchín's own story is rooted in *dinn-ghrá,* or love of one's own place.

"There is so much in Limerick that I am proud of, that I value - its sense of tradition, its Gaelic background which is still quite strong in the county, its hurling, its literary heritage, its many historic towns and villages, its lovely variety of scenery". He goes on: "And of course, its people. I think Limerick people are friendly, hospitable and tolerant, with wide interests, but still firmly rooted in their own tradition. There is nothing clannish about them."

Mainchín's long life has been dominated by a passionate interest in the Irish language, stretching from his early days in national school in Bruree, through his involvement with Conradh na Gaeilge, his long association with the Irish college in Carrigaholt and his work with Glór na nGael. He has also played a considerable role in reviving interest in the Maigue poets through Féile na Máighe, and was one of the founders of the annual weekend school in Kilfinane which honours the scholarly Joyce brothers.

And it was this dual interest - in local history and in Gaelic culture - which led in 1990 to an honorary doctorate from the National University of Ireland.

> "I have a very strong sense of place. Living so long in Limerick I feel so much a part of the place, so much sympathy with it, I can't imagine myself, given a choice, going to any other part of the country."

Given his considerable literary output, it is sometimes hard to realise that Mainchín also had a "day-job", beginning as a clerk with Limerick County Council in 1941 when he took the bus from Bruree every morning and home again in the evening. During the war years, with petrol rationing, he sometimes had to do the journey by bicycle.

His writing dates from the early 1940s when he began to contribute to *The Irish Press* and other national newspapers. A weekly column in the *Limerick Leader* under the pseudonym An Mangaire Súgach soon followed, probably the longest-running, continuous column in Ireland.

The books however followed - the first, in Irish, in 1965, on Seán South; a book on the Maigue Country, also in Irish; histories of Bruree, Kilmallock, Dromin/Athlacca, of the Joyce brothers of Glenosheen; the much-acclaimed *Portrait of Limerick* and *The Irish Quotation Book.* He is currently working on a study of the Bruree-Corcomohide (Castletown) area. A book of memoirs is also planned.

Undoubtedly, these memoirs will contain some of his many stories about Éamon de Valera, a neighbour, contemporary and friend of his mother, about the great political rallies of his youth; about his correspondence with many interesting and eminent characters over the years. One night Bruree starred in a national broadcast quiz and one contestant was asked *"Cérbh é An Mangaire Súgach?"*. The reply came back niftily: "Mainchín Seoighe." And although the quiet-spoken and courteous Mainchín is quick to discount any similarity with the original Mangaire Súgach, the poet and rake, Aindréas MacCraith, he still chuckles at the story.

In conversation with Norma Prendiville

Kieran Sheahan

When Kieran Sheahan visits his home town of Askeaton, his relatives tease him that he should have stayed there to work in the Arena petrol station and supermarket, which is owned by three of his brothers. In fact, he did work there briefly twenty years ago, after he sat his Leaving Certificate examination, but he soon embarked on a career that led him to Brussels, where he is now the managing director of Partners in Europe (PIE), a multi-million pound company which he co-founded.

As well as its headquarters in Brussels, PIE has a network of offices in Europe and the US, and a representative in Tokyo. The company acts for US and Far Eastern computer companies operating in the European market. "What distinguishes PIE is that it works like one subsidiary company, shared simultaneously by a limited number of partner companies, taking on the identity, practices and philosophies of each company when acting on its behalf in Europe," explains Kieran. PIE has grown rapidly - the turnover in 1995 was IEP 36 million, six times the 1994 turnover.

It was to Wyeth in Askeaton that he went to work that summer of 1976, as a purchasing clerk. This was a crucial decision, not only for his career, but also for his personal life, because working at Wyeth as a secretary was Mary Horan of Glin. Mary was from a sporting background - her family won many prizes for their greyhounds in Markets Field and elsewhere - and liked to attend GAA football matches. Kieran too attended Glin vs. Askeaton matches. Suffice it to say that things developed from there, and their first date was to that Limerick city landmark, the Savoy Theatre in Bedford Row.

They duly married and now have four children. Kieran refers to his eldest two (Kieran and Mark, both born in the Regional Maternity Hospital on the Ennis Road) as their "Irish children" and the younger two, daughters Aisling and Maria-Christina, as their "Belgian children" since they were born after he and Mary moved to Brussels.

While in Wyeth, he attended evening classes at the Limerick College of Art, Commerce and Technology (since renamed RTC Limerick), and was awarded a diploma by the Irish Institute of Purchasing and Materials Management. After three and a half years in Wyeth he moved to Boart Hardmetals in Shannon as a purchasing officer. "After two years, I was headhunted from there by Wang Laboratories in 1982 as a senior buyer," Kieran recalls.

While with Wang, he spent time in Limerick, the US, the UK and finally Brussels, where he was the European purchasing manager for ten countries. During his time with Wang in Limerick, he studied with the Open University through the Plassey Management and Technology Centre, and received the Open University Diploma in Management. He continued his links with the Open University while in Belgium, and studied for his MBA.

> "The key to success? Common sense! It's amazing how many people forget to use it!"

The prized MBA scroll was given to his mother, to whom he was particularly close, as he was the youngest of six children, and his father had died when he was eleven years old. "I would attribute all my success to the two women in my life; my mother, who encouraged me in my earlier years, and my wife Mary, who continues to stand by me in everything I do".

In 1993 he set up PIE with three other friends, following a discussion around a ping-pong table in the basement of his house. "It was the only free table we could find," he says. That same table has since been brought back to Shannon to take pride of place in the conference room of PIE's European Sales and Distribution Centre, established there in August 1996.

In conversation with Anna Nolan

Paul Sheane

When Shannon Development's Chief Executive Paul Sheane first joined the company in 1980, he thought he would be coming to the area for two or three years at most. "And we came to live in the area with some trepidation, because neither my wife, Heather, nor I knew anybody here," he remarks. "Sixteen years later we are still here and very happy."

It was certainly a bit of a contrast from his previous jobs in Kenya and Zambia, where he had worked in the mines and on tea plantations, as an engineer. He also volunteered to run a veterinary clinic in the Zambia bush, mainly for cats and dogs.

The African jobs came after qualifying in Trinity as an engineer, and fulfilled a long-nursed dream of working on that continent. Before going there, he married Heather Plunkett, whom he had met while she too was at Trinity, studying for a BA Mod in English Literature and Language. "We both fell in love with Africa," he says.

In Kenya there was a lot of travelling because he was working as a consultant, and here a favourite hobby came in very useful. He had learnt to fly while a student - the flying lessons paid for by helping to build the Washington DC subway as a summer job.

In 1980 the desire to return to Ireland surfaced, and once installed in the Shannon area, Paul joined the Coonagh Flying Club, where he ended up a flying instructor.

Nowadays, his flying has largely given way to dinghy

"I had a sophisticated work location in the city, but at weekends we would take off into the bush in our landcruiser, camping in the wildest, most remote areas we could find."

sailing near Kilkishen; walking near his home in Adare or Curraghchase, the Clare Glens or Cratloe Woods; and attending concerts in the University of Limerick Concert Hall - all perfect relaxation after his work in Shannon Development, where he has been Chief Executive since 1992.

"Limerick city is the heart of the Shannon region, and I am proud of the contribution of Shannon Development to the city - our contribution to urban renewal, the development of the industrial base, the development of the National Technological Park," he comments. "I am also very conscious of the potential of Limerick as a tourist centre and proud of what has been achieved here".

In his private capacity, Paul was active in the Limerick School Project, though here Heather took the lead as a founder member. Both of their two daughters, Katherine and Anna, have attended the school. Katherine runs with Dooneen Athletics Club in Dooradoyle and Anna plays the violin in the Limerick Festival Youth Orchestra.

Meanwhile Heather, who has worked with a number of companies in the region, is now taking advantage of the telecommunications infrastructure in the region to run her own business as a teleworker from Adare.

Its a long journey from his happy childhood on a small farm in County Wicklow, via Wesley College, Trinity, the US and Africa, but Paul Sheane is very content living and working in the region.

In conversation with Anna Nolan

Dean Maurice Sirr

When Dean Maurice Sirr was first ordained to the priesthood in 1965, he was appointed to St. Mary's ... but it was on the Crumlin Road in Belfast and part of his pastoral work was ministering to prisoners in the jail there.

"In fact, I have ministered to some of the prominent names we are now hearing about during the course of the peace process".

Twenty-two years later, another St. Mary's was to play a major part in his life when he was appointed Rector of Limerick City parish, and Dean of St. Mary's Cathedral; the oldest building in Limerick City since 1168 in daily use.

Originally from County Monaghan, Dean Sirr spent seventeen years working in Drumcliffe in Sligo, before being appointed to Limerick.

"One of the reasons I found my feet so quickly here is that it became apparent shortly after I arrived, that we were going to have to begin a major restoration of the Cathedral ... the biggest of its history, and that it was very urgent because some parts of the Cathedral were becoming structurally dangerous".

A year and a half of exploratory work followed, and a massive £2.8 million restoration plan was drawn up. "Around the same time, Limerick Corporation came up with a major tourist development plan for the whole King's Island area and we were encouraged to broaden our vision of the Cathedral as part of that plan".

"One of my great memories of that time was taking part in the walk from Dublin to Limerick in 1989 with Bishop Edward Darling, as a major fundraising and awareness campaign about the work planned for the Cathedral. It raised £33,000".

The restoration plan is ongoing, but coming up with the funds is a constant headache.

> "I have a philosophy in life that the past is something you treasure and learn from ... but the present is where you are. If you cannot have some vision of the future from that stand point, well then you really should have stayed where you were."

As a churchman and ecumenist, Dean Sirr says he has never felt isolated, personally, in Limerick and has enjoyed nothing but support from the Roman Catholic clergy and people of the city.

"One of my greatest pleasures was to invite the late Bishop Newman to preach at the annual ecumenical service in the cathedral".

He is now firmly ensconced in Limerick life. His wife, Paddy, whom he first met when she sang in the choir in St. Mary's in Belfast, teaches French at Villier's school. She also taught in Glenstal when they first arrived here in 1987. They have two children, Judith and Richard.

"I've watched with great pride, how Limerick has developed in recent years, and it pleases me enormously that St. Mary's is also sharing in this fine vision for the future".

One of the great things I love about Limerick people is their passion for sport. I'm still amazed at how Limerick people, particularly women, gather in Thomondgate and speak with passion and authority about rugby; it's one of the features which really does set it apart".

In conversation with Cathy Halloran

Bill Whelan

Despite his international success in the world of music, Bill Whelan has changed little. The success of *Riverdance* alone would have been enough to permanently change the temperament and personality of lesser mortals, but fame, and its inherent levels of fortune, have made little noticeable impact on the former Crescent College boy.

As a young boy growing up in Limerick, Bill had a magnetic attraction to music and it was fellow Limerickman, Richard Harris, who gave him his first big break: "A school chum, Niall Connery, and I, wrote a piece which was selected for the moderately successful Harris film *"Bloomfield"* in 1969" and introduced the budding Whelan talent to such established songwriters as Jimmy Webb and Phil Coulter.

"I will never forget the day in August when I got a 'phone call from the recording studio in London. It was Richard Harris who said: "Is that Whelan? Listen to this!" And he played the full orchestral recording of the piece, which we had "demoed" here in Limerick, and which was to be part of the film. It was one of the happiest moments of my life".

Bill's memories of Limerick are happy ones and he, in turn, is still fondly remembered as the little lad with the friendly smile and a personality that could not go unnoticed: "No matter where I go, no matter what I do in life, Limerick always comes back to me in some way. Having been out of the area for so long, I find it a stunning place to return to. For me it provides a treasury of reminiscences; memories of

"It is one of my personal ambitions to write a piece of music as a tribute to my Limerick - hopefully, that will be in the not too distant future."

the legendary Ab Sheahan, who sold *Limerick Leaders* and supported Young Munsters with intensity; a centre of great musical wealth from which I drew much inspiration; performers such as Brian Meehan, Willie Brown, Jack Glynn, Ray Fitzgerald and Johnny Hockedy, whom I admired and aspired to their greatness in my young days".

"Limerick people appear before me in the most unlikely settings, such as recently during rehearsals for a Broadway production when a member of the cast came forward and said: 'You're Billy Whelan, aren't you? I'm Malachy McCourt, I used to live behind you in Barrington Street in Limerick'."

When this interview was being written, Bill was taking charge of Windmill Recording Studio's twenty-fifth film score and once satisfied that Mr. Bernstein had achieved the purpose of his visit to Dublin, the former law graduate would jet off to New York to begin work on the Broadway stage production of Leon Uris' *Trinity*.

An only child of the late Dave and Irene (*née* Lawlor), Bill spent his formative years in the family home at 18 Barrington Street. "My parents ran a newsagency and grocery shop in Upper William Street and were both pretty musical. My mom was a super pianist and dad, who won national honours as an oarsman with Athlunkard Boat Club, played the harmonica. One of my earliest recollections is sitting under the table hitting a biscuit tin with a wooden spoon as my mother played *'Home Sweet Home'* on the piano".

In conversation with Aidan Corr

Angela Woulfe

Artist Angela Woulfe has her Gallery at 16, Pery Square, Limerick. An old building, thick-walled it has a great feeling of peace. It is here where she is happiest ... painting. Not far away in a Georgian building, 12, Cecil Street, Angela grew up with her brothers, Tim and Joe and sister, Beth. It was a house full of activity. Her father, the late Ted Dennehy, ran his photographic business from there.

Her mother, Catherine *née* Ryan known as Kitty, loved music. She used to take the children to her mother's house and there played the piano for hours. There were always music books balancing on top of the piano and occasionally a crystal vase filled with water and a beautiful display of flowers from her grandmother's garden.

Some Sundays, Angela's parents would take the family boating from the docks at Lower Cecil Street up to Thomas' Island at the Mill, Corbally. She remembers the oars in the deep water and the swirl of water and light reflecting, early morning light on the water and trees; fading light as they rowed back to the docks, up the steps from the Shannon and home.

These are glimpses of a childhood which made the artist, a child who was an observer. As a child she knew an elderly couple, who were very dear to her, but who lived apart, whose only link to each other was through their friendship with her. From time to time, one would ask her about the other, she was very aware of their loneliness and of the bond that remained between them. Even as a young child she

"I can truthfully say that there were times when life became very difficult to bear, but I could always lose myself in my paintings."

noticed people living separate unconnected lives. Angela was also aware how everyone around her had something into which they would absorb themselves.

For Angela, painting is an expression of emotion. She has been told over and over again, that her work is therapeutic for others, as well as herself.

Angela's work represents some of the most haunting oil paintings with which we are familiar in Limerick. Her work is of that rare breed that can be truly described as enchanting, drawing the observer into its magical world and holding one there in suspended time. Her paintings span a range of areas, including land and seascapes and most unusually, the night sky. But it is perhaps her paintings of old houses that best capture the imagination. Her paintings are atmosphere and time captured.

Her work is on show at her gallery, where she has been since 1986. She held solo annual Christmas exhibitions at Todds of Limerick for a number of years prior to opening her own gallery. Angela held a solo exhibition of her work in the European Parliament at Strasbourg, during the Irish presidency in 1990. She has exhibited her work in Northern Ireland and has had her paintings hung in the Royal Hibernian Association (RHA). Her work is to be found in many prestigious collections throughout the world.

She has two children who preview all her work, Daniel, an accountant and Katherine, a solicitor.

In conversation with Katherine Woulfe

Patrons

AB Airlines, AB Shannon, Shannon Airport,
    Co. Clare
Aer Rianta International, Shannon, Co. Clare
AIB Bank, Limerick
The Arena, Askeaton, Co. Limerick
Aughinish Alumina, Askeaton, Co. Limerick
Bank of Ireland, Cork
Bank of Ireland, Limerick
Blackbird Data Systems, Limerick
Liam Burke, Press 22, Limerick
Calor Gas, Dublin
Canada Life, Blackrock, Co. Dublin
Collins Steeplejacks & Partners, Ltd.,
    Ardnacrusha, Co. Limerick
The Condon Family, Fedamore, Co. Limerick
The Corner Flag Bar, Limerick
Philip Danaher, Limerick
Rt. Rev. Edward Darling, Limerick
de Courcy Estate Agents, Limerick
Stan De Lacy, Castleconnell, Co. Limerick
DF Transport, Foynes, Co. Limerick
Diocesan Offices, Limerick
Dolmen Restaurant & Galleries, Limerick
Lord Dunraven, Adare, Co. Limerick
Estuary Fuel Limited, Limerick
Fedamore GAA Club, Fedamore,
    Co. Limerick
Desmond FitzGerald, Knight of Glin,
    Co. Limerick
Sr. M. Agnes Fitzgerald, Bruree, Co. Limerick
Fr. Tony Flannery, C.S.S.R., Limerick
Gentec Electronics, Ltd., Limerick
Gleesons (SPAR), Limerick
Golden Vale plc, Charleville, Co. Cork
Dr. Michael and Mrs. Joan Griffin, Castletroy,
    Co. Limerick
Earl & Countess of Harrington, Ballingary,
    Co. Limerick
Gerard Hartmann, Gainesville, Florida, USA
Una Heaton, Limerick
John Hunt, Junior, Howth, Co. Dublin
Liam Irwin, Limerick
James McMahon Ltd., Limerick
Jurys Hotel Group PLC, Dublin
Dermot Kelly, Castletroy, Co. Limerick
Deputy Jim Kemmy, Limerick
Leahy & O'Sullivan Solicitors, Limerick
Limerick Chamber of Commerce, Limerick
Limerick City Enterprise Board, Limerick
Limerick City Parish Parishioners, Limerick
Limerick County Board G.A.A., Limerick
Limerick Leprechauns' Rugby Club, Limerick
Limerick Travel, Limerick
M&Q Plastic Products (IRL), Ltd., Limerick

M. Cahill & Sons, Limerick
Maidenform International, Ltd., Shannon,
    Co. Clare
Audrey McCormack, Limerick
Mid-Western Health Board, Limerick
Mohawk Europa, Ltd., Shannon, Co. Clare
Molex S.A., Shannon, Co. Clare
John Moloney Motors, Limerick
Moremiles Tyre Service, Ltd., Limerick
Suzanne Murphy, Cardiff, Wales
Mr. Justice John L. Murray, Luxembourg
Murray O'Laoire Associates, Limerick
Richard Nash & Co., Newcastle West,
    Co. Limerick
Gina Niland, Mungret, Co. Limerick
O'Brien Press, Dublin
Very Rev. Terence O'Brien, P.P., Limerick
Loretta O'Brien, Ardnacrusha, Co. Limerick
Pat O'Connor Victualler, Limerick
Dr. Brendan O'Reagan, Newmarket-on-
    Fergus, Co. Clare
Micheál Ó Suilleabháin &
    Nóirín Ní Ríain, Newport, Co. Tipperary
Senator Jan O'Sullivan, Limerick
Open Management Training (OMT), Limerick
Pfizer Ireland, Ltd., Dublin
Process Engineering, Limerick
Bernard & Brian Quinn, Limerick
Rand McNally Media Services, Shannon,
    Co. Clare
James Reidy & Co., Limerick
River Deep Mountain High, Limerick
Ted Russell, Limerick
Tom Ryan, Ashbourne, Co. Meath
Mainchín Seoighe, Kilmallock, Co. Limerick
Annette & Pat Shanahan, Limerick
Shannon Development, Shannon, Co. Clare
Shannon Heritage & Banquets, Bunratty,
    Co. Clare
Shannon RFC, Limerick
Kieran Sheahan, Brussels, Belgium
Southern Comedy Theatre Co., Lough Gur,
    Co. Limerick
St. Louis Irish Arts, St. Louis, MO, USA
Tiernan Properties, Limerick
Tipperary Natural Mineral Water, Co., Ltd.,
Borrisoleigh, Co. Tipperary
Tony Connolly (Limerick), Ltd., Limerick
TSB Bank, Dublin
Ulster Bank, Limerick
Western Avionics Ltd., Shannon, Co. Clare
Bill & Denise Whelan, Dublin
The Whitehouse Bar, Limerick
Woodlands Hotel, Adare, Co. Limerick

egulati
The Bo
amp